Painting Wargaming Figures: WWII in the Desert

Painting
Wargaming Figures

WWII in the Desert

Andy Singleton

Pen & Sword
MILITARY

First published in Great Britain in 2019 by
Pen & Sword Military
An imprint of
Pen & Sword Books Ltd
Yorkshire – Philadelphia

ISBN 978 1 52671 631 6

Printed and bound in India by Replika Press Pvt. Ltd.

Pen & Sword Books Limited incorporates the imprints of Atlas, Archaeology, Aviation, Discovery, Family History, Fiction, History, Maritime, Military, Military Classics, Politics, Select, Transport, True Crime, Air World, Frontline Publishing, Leo Cooper, Remember When, Seaforth Publishing, The Praetorian Press, Wharncliffe Local History, Wharncliffe Transport, Wharncliffe True Crime and White Owl.

For a complete list of Pen & Sword titles please contact

PEN & SWORD BOOKS LIMITED
47 Church Street, Barnsley, South Yorkshire, S70 2AS, England
E-mail: enquiries@pen-and-sword.co.uk
Website: www.pen-and-sword.co.uk

Or
PEN AND SWORD BOOKS
1950 Lawrence Rd, Havertown, PA 19083, USA
E-mail: Uspen-and-sword@casematepublishers.com
Website: www.penandswordbooks.com

Contents

Acknowledgements vi

Introduction vii

Part One: Basics I

    Chapter 1: Tools of the Trade
              (and some basic techniques) 3

    Chapter 2: Boot Camp 25

Part Two: Painting Guides 35

    Chapter 3: Painting the British and
              Commonwealth Army 37

    Chapter 4: Painting the Italian army 59

    Chapter 5: Painting the United States Army 83

    Chapter 6: Painting the German Army 107

    Chapter 7: Camouflage Uniforms.. 131

    Chapter 8: Basing 143

Appendix: List of Manufacturers 155

Acknowledgements

I would like to thank everyone at The Plastic Soldier Company, Perry Miniatures and Warlord Games for their assistance with this project. My deepest thanks go to my friends and family for their unceasing and invaluable support throughout writing this book, and finally a special mention must go to my friend John Lambshead, for convincing me to begin this project in the first place!

Introduction

Welcome to *Painting Wargaming Figures: WWII in the Desert*. As the title hopefully suggests, this book covers some techniques and tips used for assembling and painting figures for your wargaming use. Revolutionary, I know, given the obscurity of the title.

To first give some context regarding this book, I think it's probably necessary to mention first who it is aimed at. I've been working as a full-time commission painter for several years now, and been modelling as a hobby for most of my life. In this time I have noticed the same questions being raised frequently regarding what tools are needed, which glues are necessary for differing materials, how best to assemble models, what colours to use, and a myriad of others.

Whilst these questions are often raised by those new to the hobby, they also present the kind of information that can be helpful to any of us, as a new perspective so often is. In the main though, I've produced this book to be of most use to those with no, or at most an entry level, of modelling knowledge, so I cover a selection of the most important tools, techniques and materials before progressing into painting guides for each of the major formations in the desert campaigns of the Second World War.

The bulk of this book is spread across five painting guides, one each for the British and Commonwealth, Italians, Germans and Americans, as well as a smaller guide covering the painting of camouflage clothing. Each of these chapters further splits into three different painting parts, conscript level, regular level and finally elite level.

Conscript level is intended to be a very quick and simple guide, that you can use to either work through a mass of figures quickly, or to gain confidence in using the differing techniques before progressing to the regular and elite-level finishes. The regular level, is intended to provide you with the tools to paint figures to a pleasing level of finish, whilst also remaining reasonably quick and efficient to get through significant numbers of models. Finally, the elite level finish is the most time consuming set of techniques; however, it will give you some very fine-looking figures as a reward for your hard work.

Across each of these guides I have attempted to mix in as many combinations and variations of techniques as I could think to apply, and to present you with as many options to try out as possible. None of these techniques are limited to one force either, and can be used at will.

With regards to paint, I've predominantly listed Vallejo and Army Painter products for no other reason than they are what I use and am comfortable with. I did consider adding a conversion table to other ranges, however this runs the risk of ending up out of date, and I'd rather let the photos give you a guide to what types of colours to be using beyond those listed in the stages.

Most of the figures painted in this book are 28mm sized models, with a scattering of 20mm thrown in for good luck. This is partly down to ease of photography, and partly down to them being ranges I'm fond of. The guides should, however, work with figures of any size, and are intended to translate across different scales without too many changes. You may feel a need to tweak things slightly, but I'm pretty confident they should all work as presented here... famous last words perhaps.

A key part of finishing a figure is the basing, a poorly finished model with a smart base can still look stunning, and conversely, a nicely done piece can find some lacklustre basing really detracts from the overall appearance. Fortunately, with the desert we have a few very simple techniques that can bring the bases to life for only a minimal amount of work, so we'll be covering that after the painting guides and I'll demonstrate a mix of different tips and tricks for you to take to your basing projects.

The difference between collecting a force for wargaming, and scale modelling, is that as a gamer you will probably need to make a fair few similar models, and typically infantry will be the bulk of your hobby needs. At the start of a project this can be quite daunting, so staying motivated to actually get your force done, regardless of the level of paint finish or personal experience that you have can be a challenge. I've managed to pick up short cuts and pointers I'll be sharing, so I hope they can be enlightening.

The final part of the book will cover a list of manufactures and the sizes of models that they produce. This is by no means comprehensive, and by its nature obviously can't cover new releases added after publication. I'll cover as many manufactures as I can think of though, and cover a few different sizes of figures too.

So, who is this book aimed at? I suppose anyone really. This isn't a guide to give you top award-winning paint jobs, but might teach you some tools to get there with some experimentation. What it is really intended for, however, is to be another tool in your tool box to paint armies to an eye-pleasing wargaming standard, and to enable you to do so in a way that won't take you an age to complete either - well, hopefully anyway.

PART I
BASICS

Tools of the Trade
(and some basic techniques)

Before we come to the full painting guides, we need to cover some basics. At first glance (and a fair few later glances too), the array of tools, glues, paints and techniques varies between staggering and simply overwhelming. To help you begin to make some sense of this, I'll give a quick overview of some of the essentials, and what they can bring to your hobby sessions.

With such a huge range of paints and tools on the market, covering them all isn't really practical, but I'll cover some of the more popular ones. I'll try to cut through some of the technical terminology too, and at least give a description of what is required for a few of the most commonly used techniques.

Tools, pieces and glues: everything we'll need.

Broadly speaking, with any tools you're better off buying better-quality, more-expensive tools; with the vast majority of cases you really do get what you pay for. It's generally worth checking out a few reviews or asking around your friends too, to determine if a product perfectly fits your needs.

PLASTIC, METAL OR RESIN?

Wargaming figures are supplied in several different materials, with plastic and metal being by far the most common and resin used to a far lesser extent (though it is very common for vehicles).

Plastic figures are typically provided on a frame, called a sprue, from which they need to be removed. Traditionally, 20mm-sized plastic figures often come in a soft, polythene type of plastic And these require a good scrubbing with warm water and washing up liquid before painting, though an increasing amount of ranges are being produced in a hard plastic which is a more resilient

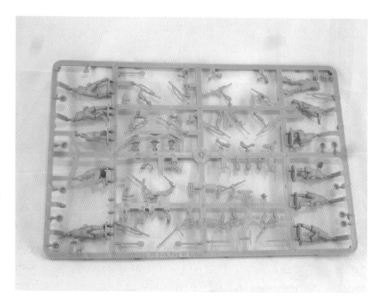

Plastic figures on a sprue.

An unassembled metal figure straight out of the pack.

material, and much easier to paint over too. 28mm and recently 15mm-sized figures are most commonly a hard plastic. Many manufacturers of figures provide each figure in several pieces to allow you some variety in posing of the figures, and I'll go into more detail in assembling these in the next chapter.

Probably the most common materials for the production of wargames figures, however, are several types of lead-free metal. These are usually supplied as single-piece castings, and typically come with a small stand attached to the figures' feet to aid placing them on their bases. Both plastic and metal figures can have moulding lines along their sides and bases, as a by-product of the production process that will need to be removed. This is a simple task and requires scraping along the line with the blunt side of a blade or quick sanding down with some files; again, I'll cover that a little later too.

Metal models require assembling with superglue or equivalent, and larger models such as artillery guns will require a degree of patience as they can quickly become somewhat frustrating if you try to rush putting them together. Patience and test fitting will always pay off here.

KNIVES, CUTTERS AND FILES

The first thing you'll need to do, unsurprisingly, is to get the component parts of your figure ready for assembly, and clean away any residue from the manufacturing process. This can take several forms, but the most common are flash and mould lines, which form when the model is being cast in its mould, and these appear as either prominent lines around a figure, or as chunks or 'worms' of excess material, especially on edges and undercuts of the figure. These casting imperfections can appear in any material, and removing them will massively improve the appearance of the finished model, especially when you are using the dry brush techniques.

Naturally, this requires some decent tools. I'd caution against using a machete and instead suggest getting some purpose-designed hobby tools instead. These can vary between prices that appear too good to be true (and generally are), to small fortunes.

Hobby Knife

These broadly fall into two types: those with various interchanged blades, such as the ubiquitous X-Acto hobby knife, and the Stanley knife. Either one of these will probably be your most frequently used tool in preparing your figures, as the sharp side of the blade can be used for cutting things, whilst the blunt (revolutionary!) edge can be used to remove mould lines by simple scraping it down them a few times.

Which type of knife you get is entirely up to you, but I'd recommend one of each, especially as they can be found pretty much anywhere that sells tools or hobby supplies for good prices. The various blades of the X-Acto style allow

Using an X-Acto knife to remove flash.

different styles and shapes of blade to be fitted, as well as allowing you to simply replace the blade once it becomes dull. The slender, sharp blades do have their limits however, they can blunt quickly when working with metal, and may struggle with cutting through thicker plastic sprues as well. For heavier duty work, the Stanley knife will do you good service, and is affordable enough to be disposable too.

Side Cutters

Also known as 'sprue cutters', these are vaguely similar to scissors, but with a shorter blade and more powerful, tensioned action. As the name cunningly suggests, these are good at cutting things and they're perfect for removing plastic parts from their carrying sprue. It's best to cut the part leaving a small stub of plastic that you can then trim with a knife or file. Also handy for metal, these can be used for removing casting lugs or parts from moulding blocks. Sprue cutters can be found in the majority of model shops, both on and offline.

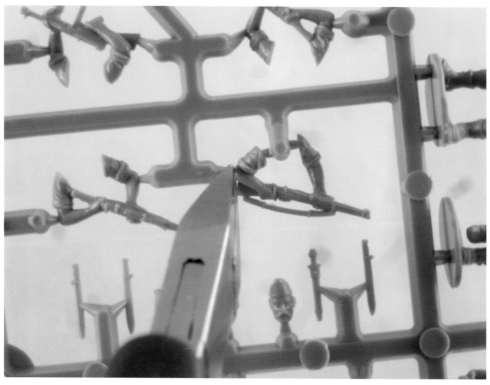

Clipping off a part of arms.

Files

Files are another immensely useful tool, and can be found in most tool/hardware shops, as well as in model and hobby shops. Ideally, what you want is a set of jeweller's files, or needle files. These typically come in sets containing several different files, each being a different shape to allow the cleaning of most parts of a model. A file with a blade more than a centimetre wide will probably prove to be too big for modelling purposes, so aim for something quite fine. These are great tools for removing mould lines and getting rid of the contact points of sprue gates.

A selection of needle files.

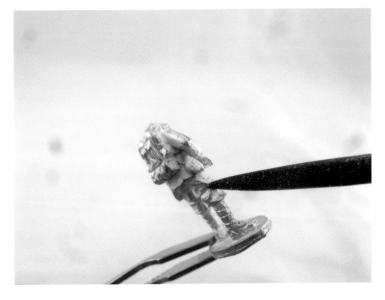

Filing off a mould line.

GLUES

Now that we have established what the figures are made from, and have trimmed and cleaned the parts, it's time to start sticking things together. For this, we'll need to ensure we are matching the correct bonding

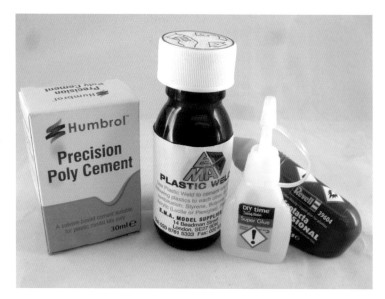

An assortment of glues.

agent to the right material. Very broadly speaking, the most commonly encountered glues are PVA, superglue, cement and solvent. PVA is a sticky paste and fine for attaching the basing materials to your figures bases, but is pretty useless for actually sticking your figures together.

Superglue, or cyanoacrylate to use its proper name, is a rapid curing cement that bonds most materials. Given the rapidity of the bonding process, superglue works best when used in small, controlled areas. I tend to apply it with a cocktail stick or equivalent, and apply small dabs to each part that will be bonded. It's better to get the parts joined, and then come back and carefully add more superglue if you feel the bond needs it, than to flood an area that will take forever to dry, and potentially make a terrible mess of your model too.

Adhesives for plastics such as those from Revell, Tamiya and Humbrol are all solvent-based, to varying degrees, and have a fairly wide range of drying times. In addition, there are also solvents designed with modelling in mind, such as Plastic Weld, which are far more potent products. All of these function on the basis of partially melting the two bonding surfaces of plastic into a very strong bond. They won't, bond metal, resin, or plastic to metal or resin. For this you will still need superglue.

Finally, we have cements. These typically come supplied in tubes, and are very sticky and foul smelling. Whilst eventually they can give a decent bond, they are for the most part quite inferior to the purpose-designed adhesives already mentioned, and should probably be avoided.

PAINT, PRIMER AND SPRAY CANS

Once our model is built, we can start to paint it. Before we can look at some techniques, though, I should probably cover a few key types of paint and paint products on the market.

In most of these guides I will be referring to using primers and spray cans, especially for the first steps of each guide.

First off, primers are probably the most important type of paint you can get, especially when working with resin or metal. These differ from paint, in being specially formulated to give a hard-wearing coat that gives a resilient

Different types of paint.

surface for handling and painting. With most paints for wargaming being water-based, this is especially important as repeated handling without a primer can cause paint to wear off a finished model. Primers typically come in black, white, grey and dark red, and I prefer to get them from places selling car body paints. If you have an airbrush, there is also a selection of good primers on the market for these, but time and space constraints mean I'll avoid discussing airbrushes in this book.

When working with purely plastic models, you can get away with using coloured spray paints as the initial layer of colour. There are a great, great many of these on the market in both enamel and acrylic form, so finding something to fit your needs shouldn't be too hard. Notable ranges though are The Army Painter, Plastic Soldier Company, Tamiya and Humbrol. When working with metal or resin models I suggest applying a light coating of primer and allowing this to dry thoroughly (for at least 12 hours, better 24 hours though).

By far the vast majority of paints used for wargaming are acrylic. These are water soluble, but quick drying and hard wearing. When purchased, most paints, such as those from the Vallejo Model Colour range, require some thinning to get the best results, as paint that is too thick will not only be difficult to get where you want it to go, but it may also swamp the detail on your model. To thin your paint, simply apply a little to a pallet (an old tile or plastic lid is great for this) then add an equal amount of water and stir together using an old brush. For best results, add a tiny amount of flow improver, this will hold the coverage of the paint together well, whilst still keeping the paint controllable.

You may also encounter enamel paints. These are an oil-based product, and whilst useful, especially for basing and weathering applications on vehicles, are of less use to us in getting our armies finished as the drying times are considerably longer than with acrylics. They also require more specialized cleaning and thinning products.

PAINT BRUSHES AND CARE

So, with all this discussion of tools, I suppose paint brushes might be a good item to mention in a book on figure painting! As with most tools, brushes vary between super cheap, where you get a pack of a dozen brushes for a few pounds, up to fine Kolinsky sable brushes that can seem hugely expensive in comparison. As someone who paints a huge amount of models, it's worth splashing out on the best quality brushes you can afford. Not only will they last longer and work out cheaper in the long term but a high quality brush will also give you better brush control and results.

Personally my favourites are the Winsor & Newton series 7, though for the more affordable end of the spectrum Pro Arte, Army Painter and Games Workshop all produce useful brushes. It's worth having some cheap,

A variety of brushes.

An old, worn brush like this still has its uses.

A good-quality, Size I brush like this is the workhorse of painting.

disposable brushes too, for jobs like mixing paint, applying washes, dry-brushing and applying glue, anything you do not want to use your best brushes for.

Paint brushes are typically made from either synthetic weave or natural hair. Synthetic brushes don't tend to hold paint as well as natural brushes but this isn't too much of a hindrance when working with acrylics as you will be cleaning the brush anyway, thanks to the rapid drying times of the paint. However, natural brushes do tend to give you better control over the application of paint. Natural brushes are better at retaining their point for precision application, and also hold more paint, giving the added benefit of being able to keep working on a subject for longer. Natural fibre bristles are at their best when used for detail work, especially painting areas such as faces or fine, layered highlights.

As you work, you will naturally need to clean your brush. When using most acrylic paints a simple pot of water will be sufficient for use between changing colours and to prevent paint drying in the bristles, and regardless of what your brush's bristles are made from I'd not recommend leaving it any longer than a few minutes between giving it a quick swish around in some water.

For more long-term care, there is a wide range of brush cleaners and conditioners on the market, and frequently there are products put out from each of the major paint ranges. It's worth investing in either a cleaner or, better yet, some brush soap to prevent excess wear or damage to your brushes' bristles. Each of these products will have their own set of specific instructions, usually printed on the side of the packaging, typically involving giving the brush a solid swishing around in the cleaner/soap, leaving it to stand for a bit and then rinsing clean and shaping. I've used a combination of brush soap and high-end sable brushes to keep the same fine brushes in use nearly every day for four years now!

With regards to what size and shape brush you should be getting, a size 0, a size 1 and a size 2 round should be sufficient. There are several ranges that have miniature bristles on the market, and these tend to hold less paint than conventionally sized brushes. They are useful for tiny details such as eyes or certain camouflage patterns, but a good quality standard round brush will give you better overall control.

You'll probably spot in the painting guides the use of flat brushes, and these are just what it sounds like, a flat, chisel-like brush. These are great for dry-brushing as they have a good amount of control, and lend themselves well to pulling over the raised detail, allowing you to have fairly precise highlights quickly. They aren't compulsory for dry brushing, but do make life a lot easier.

This size ½ flat-head brush is handy for dry-brushing.

DRY-BRUSHING

Over the course of the painting guides, I'll be referring to several techniques. Rather than repeat myself in each guide, I'll cover a few of the basic ones here, so they are ready for you to add to your toolbox.

Dry-brushing is, as the name implies, the technique of using a small amount of paint on a dry brush, to build up layers of colour by quickly flicking the brush over the surface of the model. This will have the effect of adding a contrasting colour to raised areas, whilst leaving the remaining parts of the figure in shade.

Whilst simple in concept, it can take a little practice to really become proficient with dry brushing. Foremost, one must endeavour to keep the brush you are using as dry as possible. Once your paints are applied to the pallet, avoid thinning them, and just load up the tip of the brush with a tiny amount of paint.

Loading the dry brush with paint.

Clean this paint from the brush with some tissues, then test to see how much paint is present by lightly dragging the bristles over some card or an old figure.

You want the paint to be landing on the tops of creases, folds and details of the model, but also want to avoid streaking or blobbing of paint. With dry-brushing it's best

Removing paint from the dry brush.

Dry-brushing the figure's jacket.

to allow several layers of paint to build up gradually to achieve the effect you are aiming for, as opposed to going in with one initial, heavy dry brush as this can overwhelm your model.

LAYERING

Layering is a somewhat labour intensive way to add highlights and shade to our figures, and essentially is simply the process of painting in contrasting colours to create the illusion of depth and shade. You'll need to

Adding paint to the palette.

Adding water to paint to thin the paint.

19

*Using a size 1
brush to apply a
layered highlight.*

thin your paint a little more than you would usually; it's hard to give a precise mix of ratios, but by eyeballing it you want something fairly thin, but that won't flood the model.

Just load up your favourite brush for detail work, and start to apply the paint to anywhere on the model that catches the light. To get the most natural look, pick a direction for the light to be directed from, and use this to guide where your highlights or shadows land.

For more eye-catching highlights, keep applying increasing amounts of ever-lighter highlights to the model, applying the highlight to only the highest, and most prominent areas of detail.

WASHING AND GLAZING

A wash is a heavily thinned paint, applied so that it flows and settles in the details of the model. These can

Applying a wash to an Italian's backpack.

be purchased as ready mixed forms, or you can make your own. To make your own, simply add two or three parts of water, with a little washing up liquid, to one part paint, then mix these together. Paint this solution over the figure, allowing this to run into recesses and details, though trying not to allow the wash to pool. This can be caused by too much wash being applied, and thus flooding the model.

A glaze is a similar technique to a wash, and is used to unify the highlights and shades already applied. The process is largely the same as applying a wash but it is applied far more sparingly. Simply use a less-heavily loaded brush than you would for a wash and paint this over the model, allowing the colour of the glaze to form on the figure, but without flowing into the recesses as heavily as a wash would. This is a very subtle technique, and is likely to be one of the last techniques you apply to a figure.

Varnishing some feathers.

VARNISH

A varnish is a clear, protective layer applied to the model to protect the paint finish during handling, especially when transporting and during games. For our purposes, the most useful varnishes are gloss and matt finishes. Gloss varnishes are highly shiny, but they are also very hard wearing. Naturally, being shiny is not overly realistic for our desert-fighting models, so this brings in the use of a matt, or flat, varnish instead. Whether you use just one type of varnish, both types, or none at all is entirely up to you. Typically I choose not to varnish as it can have the effect of dulling the paint (plus I don't get to game with my models that often…) but if you're anticipating heavy use and handling then varnish is pretty much required.

Varnishes can be obtained in many forms, but most useful for our purposes are those in spray cans. Spray cans allow you to varnish many figures quickly and evenly, and also have the added bonus of generally being touch dry reasonably quickly. Avoid spraying on hot or humid days, however, as this can cause the paint to cloud and potentially ruin your paint job! Brush-applied varnish will give you more control and is far less likely to cloud or have some adverse, weather-related failing on your lovingly finished figure!

Hopefully these tips and techniques will have you feeling confident about getting on with assembling and painting your figures, and as ever should be treated as a stepping off point for your own experiments. Now on to actually building your models!

Italians ready for patrol.

Boot Camp

So, with our tools collected and our miniatures sat on the desk, it's time to start getting them ready for paint. It's simple enough to glue the bits together roughly and have at it straight away with painting but this, while potentially getting your figures ready for gaming sooner, may prove to be somewhat frustrating if components start to fall off later, gaps reveal themselves, or poses look weird and unnatural. The following tips were initially written with plastic models in mind. However, everything applies equally to metal figures, with just the required adhesives being different.

In the previous chapter we discussed the key tools that you will require for getting your models prepared and cleaned up, and this should be everything you need covered, however it's probably worth getting hold of some fine grade wet-and-dry sand paper too for cleaning up awkward shapes or particularly fine and light mould lines that may be a little tricky to go at with a file without damaging the surrounding area.

Whilst metal figures are usually single-piece models, or at most come with a separate head or limb, plastic figures, especially those in 28mm size, are frequently provided in multiple components, sometimes as many ten parts by the time you factor in their webbing and field gear. Not only is this going to be something of a slog to put together, there is also an inherent amount of potential frustration in working with so many small components, and attempting to get them to remain on a figure whilst you carry out the rest of the assembly process.

There are several steps for alleviating this however. First of all, take the time to work out a list of what you want each model in a squad to be armed and equipped with. This will ensure you don't build a load of figures that you later realize you don't need, and will help you plan out the rest of the assembly process. I highly recommend working in batches for this process too. My preference is to work in full squads, though batches of five to ten figures are also effective.

Batches of this size mean that you can complete gluing a set of parts to one figure and then work through the group. By the time you are finished with the last, the first should be dry enough for you to do the next stage of assembly with.

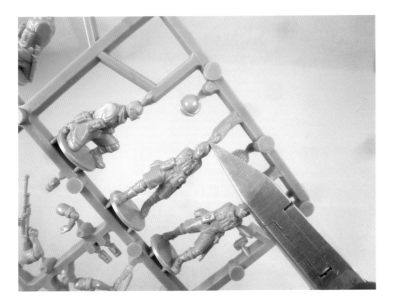

Now that you know how many figures you need, firstly
remove their bodies and (if separate) legs from the sprues,
clean up any mould lines and stick these onto the models'
bases. If you are using MDF or resin bases, you'll need to
superglue the models to those.

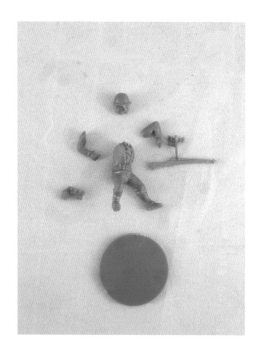

With the bodies drying, we can think about posing and equipment. It's generally easiest to add any pouches and equipment to the model at this stage before the arms are added, as they can make access difficult. Depending on how much needs adding, take a look at photos of the real soldiers, and see how they wore and placed their field gear; there were generally pretty prescribed placements for equipment.

We're now ready to start adding our figures arms. With most figures, these fall into two broad types. Either, a single component with both arms and rifle moulded together, or multiple parts consisting of individual arms and weapon as (at least) three pieces. Each method presents its own challenges, so we'll look at the single-component piece first.

Single component arm/weapon combinations are an increasingly common trend in recently designed plastic figures, and also crop up in metal sets from time to time.

This design aids massively in assembling a figure as the time and fiddliness is much reduced, and it's also much easier to visualise how a figure will look, so you are able to trim and tidy a set of arms, then match it to the various bodies you have to get the pose you like. The only negative to these is that sometimes they can also be matched to certain bodies, or at least fit better with certain torsos in a set. As a result, a certain amount of dry fitting is required, though this isn't too onerous a task, and one we're probably doing anyway to test out the poses.

For figures where the arms are split into left and right, with a separate weapon, we have to first work out roughly what the model is doing, so in this case aiming his rifle. With a rough pose decided, I like to attach the arm that is controlling the figure's weapon first, so typically the right arm. After this I attach the left, and finally the weapon. This is all done using a plastic glue, and on a figure-by-figure basis even when working in batches. By working in

this sequence we get enough time to be able to position the model in a natural way.

Now the arms are on, it's simply a matter of attaching the figure's head. Again it's worth test fitting the parts first, as sometimes the neck may need a little trimming at the base to ensure the best possible fit, without the model looking like a heavily armed giraffe. Although an easy task, the position of the head is pretty critical to the final appearance of the figure.

The head and face are pretty much always the focal point of a model, and as such need to be positioned in a way that is complimentary to the rest of the model. A figure aiming a shouldered weapon to the left, whilst glancing to the right, tells a very different story to aiming down the sights of its weapon for example.

The beauty of plastic models is that the amount of poses and armament combinations possible from even a single box is simply staggering. The sheer variety of poses

however is daunting, and I can't recommend highly enough trying out some of the poses for yourself to see if they actually work and feel 'right', as it's all too easy coming up with something that looks spectacular, until you find an arm can't actually bend that way, or there's now no room for the head to fit without some spectacular neck problems.

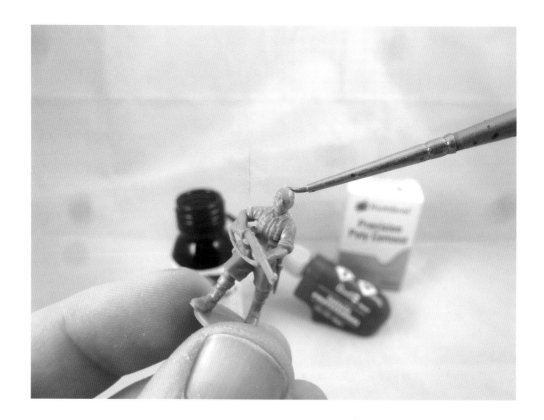

The key with plastics is patience, and using proper plastic adhesive. To take your figures up a notch, have a look through photos and footage of soldiers of the period in action, too really get a feel of how they moved and carried themselves, and you'll be able to do some spectacular stuff with plastic figures.

PART II

PAINTING GUIDES

Now that we have covered some basic tools and techniques, it's time we started some painting! As mentioned earlier, each nation's guide will be split between Conscript, Regular and Elite levels. **Conscript Level** aims to give you a smart but very quick and simply painted figure that you can take to the table top in no time. **Regular Level**, will be a balance of speed and detail, and will give you a nice looking army whilst still not requiring too much of a time investment either. Finally, the **Elite Level** of finish is aimed at creating some detailed and good looking figures for both collecting and gaming.

All of these techniques are designed to work particularly well if you decide to work in batches of models, and each step can be applied to each figure before moving on to the next stage. I'll come back to talking about batch painting when we come to the 'keeping motivated' part of this book.

Whilst broken down along national lines, any of these techniques can be utilized for any nation, by simply selecting a technique you like, with the colours used for your nation of choice. As ever, please take these guides as a jumping off point for your own painting and modelling experiments.

For most of these guides I will be using paints and shades from both the Army Painter and Vallejo ranges, and will include both the name of the paint, and product serial code. These ranges can be found in most model shops and are also readily available online. There is always going to be debate around whether a colour is most accurate or suitable for a historical model, however these are simply the ones I feel fit each nation's forces the best.

3

Painting the British and Commonwealth Army

The British Empire spanned most of the globe, and from this was drawn the truly Commonwealth Western Desert Force, and later the Eighth Army. Initially operating to protect British interests in North Africa and the Middle East, with especial significance placed upon the Suez Canal, the British and Commonwealth forces would go on to first hold, and then push back and finally drive out the Axis forces from North Africa.

Despite being thought of as a British formation, for most of its existence the Eighth Army was largely composed of personnel drawn from Australia, New Zealand, India and South Africa, As well as Poles, French and the men of the King's African Rifles.

With German aggression in Europe largely successful as of 1940, and despite the Axis' apparent dominance of the continent, Italian expansion into Egypt had largely stalled, and by the beginning of 1941 Commonwealth forces had driven the Italians from Egypt, and gone on to take significant ground in Cyrenaica, with the almost complete destruction of the Italian 10th army. The arrival of Erwin Rommel and the German Afrika Korps to serve alongside the beleaguered Italians was initially very successful. However, the Australian 9th Infantry division had withdrawn into the fortified port of Tobruk, which became a key logistical objective for the Axis forces. Tobruk was besieged between April and November 1941, and was eventually relieved following the success of Operation Crusader, which served to drive the combined German and Italian forces back out of Egypt. Through the rest of 1941 and 1942, the campaign in North Africa swung backwards and forwards across the desert, with Panzer Armee Afrika finally being broken at the Second Battle of El Alamein. This success, combined with the landings in Tunisia in November 1942, allowed the Allied forces to pursue the Axis out of Africa, across the Mediterranean, and ultimately into Italy.

By the late 1930's the British Army and its Commonwealth colleagues had been fighting in hot, dusty climates for over a century. This wealth of experience and knowledge had led to the introduction initially of a khaki service dress uniform towards the end of the nineteenth century. This uniform remained largely unchanged for the next few decades, until supplanted and eventually replaced by a lighter, looser-fitting uniform of long-sleeved shirt and shorts, and by 1941 this new uniform was commonplace, with the sleeves of the shirt commonly rolled up to around the elbow, though short sleeve shirts can also be seen. Interestingly, a type of trouser that could be folded up and worn as shorts was also issued, though these appear to have been rare.

Whilst shorts and shirt are the most familiar appearance of the Tommy in the desert, other uniform was also present. Through 1942 and 1943, additional uniforms started to arrive as War Aid from the United States, and especially towards the end of the campaign longer, khaki trousers and bush shirts were starting to appear. Most notable, however, of the additional uniform items worn, especially in the winter months, was the use of battledress. This was a heavy, thick, khaki brown-coloured wool uniform designed for the battlefields of Europe that proved popular in the cold nights and mornings of the desert. Whilst not covered in this particular guide, if you have some figures wearing battledress and are wondering how to paint them, the colours used in the United States painting guide for that figure's trousers would work equally well for battledress, as well as officers' peaked caps, as the colours were fairly similar between battledress and the US Army issue woollen trousers.

The figures I've chosen to use for this particular guide are from the Perry Miniatures set, WW 1 Desert Rats 1940-4, and these have been assembled using the techniques covered in Chapter 2: Boot Camp. My preference is to always fully assemble a model before painting, but you should always experiment to find what works best for you.

CONSCRIPT LEVEL

Step 1

So, with the figure built, it's time to start laying down some colours. For the sake of brevity I've used one of the colour primers produced by the Army Painter range. I've chosen the Skeleton Bone spray but any pale, dust colour would work very nicely. Tamiya and Humbrol both produce extensive ranges of spray paint, so you can certainly use whatever you can find locally if the Army Painter sprays are difficult to obtain.

As the figure is plastic I've not used a more traditional primer, however if I were working with a metal figure I would first give the figure a light spray of grey primer, and leave this to dry over night before coming back with the colour spray.

Paints used

Area	Colour
Whole figure	Army Painter Skeleton Bone spray

Brush: None.

Step 2

With the figure nicely dried, ideally after being allowed to dry for twenty-four hours, we can start to add in some colour to the figure. Try to be as neat as you can, as these colours will form the base for the next few stages. I would suggest using a size 1 paint brush as this will hold a good working quantity of paint, whilst still retaining a good deal of control too. We'll come back and paint the figure's weapons in a later stage.

Paints used

Area	Colour
Helmet	Vallejo **988** Khaki
Webbing and Socks	Vallejo **882** Middlestone
Skin	Vallejo **803** Brown Rose
Boots	Vallejo **862** Black Grey

Brush: Size 1.

Step 3

Now that our basic colours are in place, we can highlight the Desert Rat. As this level of finish is aimed at being quick and very simple, all that is required is a dry-brushing over the whole figure. This is done with a size ½ flat-headed brush. Whilst covered in Chapter 1: Tools of the Trade, it never hurts to reiterate that less is more when dry-brushing. Ensure your brush bristles are totally dry, and that they are only holding a very small amount of paint, then lightly dust the brush over the figure, allowing a small amount of paint to build up on the raised parts of the figure.

Highlight colours

Area	Colour
Whole Figure	Vallejo 837 Pale Sand

Brush: Flat-headed size ½.

Step 4

With the figure dry-brushed, we can now pick out his weapons and equipment. Whilst this figure is armed with a rifle, the same techniques apply to any weapons he may be carrying, though it may be worth checking with the box art and your references to ensure you are picking out the details correctly.

Coming back to the size 1 brush, and again being as tidy as possible, first pick out the weapon with a brown colour; I've used Mahogany brown, and used this to pick out the entrenching tool handle hanging from the figure's back. This is the small thing looking like a bag hanging from the centre rear of the figure's belt. Use a dark brown to pick out the bayonet scabbard hanging to the left of the figure's belt.

Certain poses will show the butt plate of the rifle, whilst others may also show a belt buckle. Whilst not necessary, especially when aiming to have a very quick and simple scheme, you can pick these out with brass too if you feel like adding an extra level to your model.

Paints used:

Area	Colour
Woodwork (rifle stock, entrenching tool)	Vallejo 836 Mahogany Brown
Metalwork	Vallejo 863 Gunmetal
Scabbard	Vallejo 871 Leather Brown
Buckles and butt plate of rifles	Vallejo 801 Brass

Brush: Size 1.

Conscript stage ready! These four steps will very quickly allow you to paint a fairly large numbers of figures, with the longest, most time-consuming tasks likely to be picking out the details and weapons, though even that should be fairly quick once you become familiar with the figures' weapons and their respective details. You are now ready to proceed to basing the figure, and deploy it into your games.

REGULAR LEVEL

This finish, whilst very similar to techniques used at the Conscript level, also requires a few subtle changes in the order that colours are applied. We will also be using some slightly different paints to reflect the new techniques that are being used.

Step 1

As with the Conscript level finish, we spray the figure all over with the colour primer, and all the above notes apply here too. As this stage is very quick, it can be a helpful time saver to spray fairly large batches in one go, and then work on these in smaller groups as you progress to the next painting stages.

Paints used:

Area	Colour
Whole figure	Army Painter Skeleton Bone spray

Brush: None.

Step 2

This is where we have our first deviation from the Conscript finish. With the figure dry and in its pale, dusty khaki colour, we will dry-brush it with some pale sand coloured paint before picking out any of the other details. This is to ensure that the dry-brushing does not leave any paint on the skin, webbing or weapon etc.

Area	Colour
Whole Figure	Vallejo 837 Pale Sand

Brush: Flat-headed size ½.

Step 3

Having dry-brushed highlights onto the models uniform, we are now able to come in and pick out the details. Neatness is important here, especially with the uniform finished. Coming back and having to neaten up the uniform is both frustrating and fairly time consuming, and not more than a little disheartening too! I've also suggested using a paler helmet colour and flesh tone for the figure than in the Conscript stage, as the wash layer that will be added in step 4 will darken those colours a little.

Area	Colour
Helmet	Vallejo 970 Buff
Webbing and Socks	Vallejo 882 Middlestone
Skin	Vallejo 955 Flat Flesh
Boots	Vallejo 862 Black Grey
Woodwork (rifle stock, entrenching tool)	Vallejo 836 Mahogany Brown
Metalwork	Vallejo 863 Gunmetal
Scabbard	Vallejo 871 Leather Brown
Skin	Vallejo 803 Brown Rose
Boots	Vallejo 862 Black Grey
Buckles and butt plate of rifles	Vallejo 801 Brass

Brush: Size 1.

47

Step 4

The figure is now starting to look the part, and is nearly ready for the table top; however, we can now really bring it to life with some selected use of ink shades. There are a great many similar products available but I'm using the Army Painter range as they have a great, easily controllable viscosity. These products can tint and darken the colours they are being applied to, hence using lighter tones for the skin and helmets, so never be afraid to experiment first on some old or spare models.

When applying these inks, treat them as you would any other paint, though they do not require anything and can be used straight from the bottle. Simply paint them over the areas you wish to be shaded, and then through capillary action the tones will flow into the recesses and provide you with some instant shading. Just be mindful not to overload your brush, as this may result in the tone pooling or running into areas you don't want it too.

Whilst I have listed four different tone shades, if you wish to simplify things you could get away with simply using the soft tone on all the areas listed instead.

Area	Colour
Helmet	Army Painter Soft Tone
Webbing, uniform and Socks	Army Painter Soft Tone
Skin	Army Painter Flesh Tone
Boots	Army Painter Strong Tone
Woodwork (rifle stock, entrenching tool)	Army Painter Dark Tone
Metalwork	Army Painter Dark Tone
Scabbard	Army Painter Soft Tone
Buckles and butt plate of rifles	Army Painter Soft Tone

Brush: Size 1.

Regular finish level is now complete! Using this process is marginally more complex than the Conscript level, and would work well if you were wishing to mark out favourite units or distinguish weapon and gun teams. If you have some figures already finished using the Conscript method, you could happily apply step 4 of this process to the figure to add some further detail and depth at a later date.

ELITE LEVEL

This is our most detailed and time-consuming finish, and can seem quite daunting. However, it will also give you some spectacular-looking models. It can take a while to get a full army finished using these methods but the end result is well worth the extra effort. If you do not want to invest the time into your rank-and-file models, this can be a nice way to mark out your officers and centrepiece items, as well as vehicle crews.

Step 1

As this is quite an in-depth paint job, we can relax at this stage and simply spray the model as with the other finish levels.

Paints used

Area	Colour
Whole figure	Army Painter Skeleton Bone spray

Brush: None.

Step 2

When the primer has dried, it's time to block in our first layer of colours. These will be the foundation of the rest of the shading and highlights to come, and are mostly familiar ones from the Conscript and Regular paint levels, however they will also be utilized somewhat differently.

Paints used

Area	Colour
Helmet	Vallejo 988 Khaki
Webbing and Socks	Vallejo 882 Middlestone
Skin	Vallejo 803 Brown Rose
Boots	Vallejo 862 Black Grey
Woodwork (rifle stock, entrenching tool)	Vallejo 836 Mahogany Brown
Metalwork	Vallejo 863 Gunmetal

Area	Colour
Scabbard	Vallejo 822 German Camo Black Brown
Skin	Vallejo 803 Brown Rose
Boots	Vallejo 862 Black Grey
Buckles and butt plate of rifles	Vallejo 801 Brass

Brush: Size 1.

Step 3

To begin adding some interest and life to the model, we will start painting layers of highlights on to the figure. Rather than dry-brushing, we will use the layering method from Chapter 1, as this will allow us to have more control and create a subtler finish. These first highlights do not need to be too neat, as later stages will tidy the model, but it's still worth being crisp as you can with them.

First Highlight colours

Area	Colour
Helmet	Vallejo 970 Buff
Uniform	Vallejo 837 Pale Sand
Webbing and Socks	Vallejo 970 Buff
Skin	Vallejo 955 Flat Flesh
Boots	None
Woodwork (rifle stock, entrenching tool)	981 Orange Brown
Metalwork	None
Boots	None
Buckles and butt plate of rifles	None

Brush: Size 0.

Step 4

Step 4 is largely optional, as we are adding a second highlight layer to the figure. My preference is to do this as it helps to add a level of richness to the final model, as well as helping to make the contrast of the highlights much more vibrant. It can end up being deceptively time consuming though, so can be skipped if you prefer.

These highlights are painted onto the very lightest parts of the figure, so edges of pockets, tops of sleeves, fingertips and knuckles, and anywhere else that naturally catches the light.

We'll also add some 5 o'clock shadow to the face using a light grey paint. This is applied as any other layered highlight, though restricted to the lower part of the model's face.

Second Highlight colours

Area	Colour
Helmet	None
Uniform	Vallejo 918 Ivory
Webbing and Socks	Vallejo 837 Pale Sand
Skin	Vallejo 815 Basic Skin Tone
Stubble	Vallejo 986 Deck Tan
Boots	Vallejo 995 German Grey
Woodwork (rifle stock, entrenching tool)	None
Metalwork	None
Buckles and butt plate of rifles	None

Brush: Size 0.

Step 5

It's worth leaving the figure to dry for a few hours, preferably overnight, before coming back and applying the shading tones as they can damage your highlights if the paint hasn't fully dried.

As the figure has a fairly pale uniform, my preference is to use a soft tone ink, however if you like a bit more contrast you can use the strong tone ink. Alternatively, if you wish the figure's webbing to have more contrast with the uniform you could use strong tone over this to distinguish it.

It's worth taking a little time and experimenting to find a finish that appeals to you. You can also use the different shades to add a little variation to a squad's uniforms. This will allow you to represent newer, less-faded equipment. Painting a few figures with a strong tone shade on their uniforms within a squad that is mostly painted with soft tone can add some subtle variety, and make the figures appear to be new replacements, or at least freshly dressed!

Area	Colour
Helmet	Army Painter Soft Tone
Uniform	Army Painter Soft Tone
Webbing and Socks	Army Painter Soft Tone
Skin	Army Painter Flesh Tone
Boots	Army Painter Strong Tone
Woodwork (rifle stock, entrenching tool)	Army Painter Dark Tone
Metalwork	Army Painter Dark Tone
Scabbard	Army Painter Soft Tone
Buckles and butt plate of rifles	Army Painter Soft Tone

Brush: Size 1.

Step 6

Although the figure has had several highlights applied, and also had a nice level of depth added with the shading tones, by applying a final level of small, spot highlights you will make the model really spring to life. When applying the tones, they both pull colours together and help to unify a model, but they do also dull down the brightest of your highlights as well. To apply this layer, use your finest brush, and apply small areas of colour on the most prominent parts of the figure. Holding the figure under your light can be a very easy way to see where these points fall depending on the pose of your figure.

Final Highlight colours

Area	Colour
Helmet	Vallejo 970 Buff
Uniform	Vallejo 918 Ivory
Webbing and Socks	Vallejo 837 Pale Sand
Skin	Vallejo 815 Basic Skin Tone
Stubble	Vallejo 986 Deck Tan
Boots	Vallejo 995 German Grey
Woodwork (rifle stock, entrenching tool)	981 Orange Brown
Metalwork	None
Buckles and butt plate of rifles	None

Brush: Size 00.

Elite-level figure finished! As you can probably tell, this is a time-consuming process. However, when broken down over a group of five to ten figures it can still be carried out in a fairly decent amount of time, though this largely comes down to how much you enjoy painting and how quickly you want to get gaming with your

models. A full army painted this way will always attract positive comment, but these techniques, as with those of the regular painting level, could be reserved for your favourite and fanciest figures.

4

Painting the Italian army

Italy declared war on Britain and France in June 1940, with the aim of expanding the Italian African Empire which had been steadily growing since the 1890s. With the Italian African Empire consisting of Ethiopia, Eritrea and the Somaliland, the Italian war aims were to secure the Mediterranean Sea whilst also claiming territories within the Balkans and Middle East. The lynchpin of this plan was for the British and allied forces to be driven out of Egypt, allowing the securing of the Suez Canal and Palestinian Oil fields, thus severely hampering allied lines of communication and supply.

In the summer of 1940 the Italian army was large, and had gained experience fighting in numerous colonial

actions, as well the Spanish Civil war and 1939 invasion of Albania. By 1941 the forces in Africa appeared impressive on paper, with nearly a quarter of a million troops, more than 300 tanks and supported by sizeable numbers of artillery and aircraft. Troop quality varied widely though, from fragile and unproven to hardened and experienced veterans.

The large variety of Italian vehicles and weapons present were mostly suitable for colonial policing actions rather than facing off against a modern, well-equipped European power and consisted of machine gun-armed tankettes, First World War vintage artillery and only a minimal amount of transport vehicles and radios. Mobility proved to be a huge issue for the Italians, and as the campaign in the desert continued this severely hampered their capabilities in prosecuting attacks and reacting in defensive situations. What armoured vehicles were present in the theatre were notoriously mechanically unreliable. However, they performed efficiently when deployed well, though command and control issues persisted due again to limited radio equipment.

Despite these issues, the Italian army in the desert comprised the bulk of Axis forces for the entirety of the campaign, even after the arrival of the Deutsches Afrika Korps, and the Italian soldier served bravely and stubbornly when well led.

As a long-time colonial power, Italy had created a range of practical and useful tropical uniforms, with the most widespread being a copy of their Continental uniform, manufactured in a khaki material rather than field grey wool. In addition to this, shorts or trousers were equally popular, as were several types of Sahariana bush jackets; again, all of these where in the same khaki colour, and when the trouser was worn, this was often bound by field grey puttees.

Helmets were issued in a green grey colour, however they were frequently repainted with sand paint to match the desert conditions. In the early part of the campaign, and especially by Bersaglieri, tropical pith helmets were worn, and these were issued in a pale khaki colour, with the Bersaglieri issued items adorned with black Cockerel feathers.

Boots were black leather with enlisted men wearing grey leather field gear, whilst officers wore brown leather belts.

The figures were are going to be using for the Italian guide are all from Warlord Games' 28mm Bersaglieri range, and consist of metal figures. For a reminder of how to prepare metal figures, please check back with the Boot Camp chapter.

CONSCRIPT LEVEL

With this model, we are going to be using the priming layer as our figure's highlights, and then simply applying fairly thin layers of paint over this to fill in the detail. First up, however, is the priming. As detailed in Chapter 1 (Tools of the Trade), we want to use an enamel-based primer and give a good even covering to the whole figure. This may require a few light coats as we need the entire figure to be covered.

Step 1

Paints used

Area	Colour
Whole figure	White car primer

Brush: None.

Step 2

Having left the figure to dry for twenty-four hours or so, all that is required at this step is to apply a very thin coat of our khaki colour. This requires thinning the paint a little more than you usually need too, and applying this to the model's uniform. You don't need to be too neat but try to keep the paint away from any areas of skin.

When thinning the paint, simply apply some paint to your palette, and then add water. A roughly 50/50 mix of paint and water should be enough, though experimenting is key here. You want to have the paint at around the consistency of milk, so that when painted over the white base layer some of this shows through to create shading.

Give the uniform a few minutes to dry (I suggest grabbing a coffee), thin down your chosen flesh-colour paint using the same method, and repeat the process over any areas of skin.

If the paint ends up looking uneven or chalky, you can always apply another layer once the previous one has dried, until you get to a level of contrast that you like.

Area	Colour
Uniform	Vallejo 882 Middlestone
Skin	Vallejo 803 Brown Rose

Brush: Size 1.

Step 3

Now that the majority of the figure is painted all we need to do is paint in the colours of the various detail parts of the uniform. We don't need to thin the paint as heavily as in Step 2 either, and it can be applied normally.

Neatness is pretty critical though, as it'll be tricky to tidy up any overspill of paint.

The feathers in the figure's helmet are picked out with some black ink as this gives a nice deep and lustrous effect, though you could use any other black paint you may have.

Area	Colour
Helmet	Vallejo 976 Buff
Feathers	Vallejo Game Colour 094 Black Ink
Webbing	Vallejo 896 Basalt Grey
Pack	Vallejo 940 Saddle Brown
Rifle stock	Vallejo 836 Mahogany Brown
Metal work	Vallejo 863 Gunmetal
Putees	Vallejo 830 German Field Grey
Boots	Vallejo 862 Black Grey

Brush: Size 1.

And that's it! This is quite a simple scheme to do, but can be very effective with a little practice. Naturally waiting for the paint to dry is a little more time consuming as being that much more thinned down than usual it takes longer for the paint to fully cure. However, because of this the process is perfect for working on batches, especially larger batches of models. You could potentially do stages 1 and 2 on fairly large numbers of figures, and then break that down into smaller, more manageable groups. This will propel you through what could be quite a quite a dragging project very quickly. Conscript stage ready!

REGULAR LEVEL

The Regular level of finish will use many of the same techniques as the Conscript level, however the sequence of application is a little different, and there are a few more stages to be aware of. Again, we're starting off with a smart, tidy all-over coat of white primer, then putting the figure aside to dry for twenty-four hours.

Step 1

Paints Used

Area	Colour
Whole figure	White car primer

Brush: None.

Step 2

Here we start to fill in the uniform colours; unlike in the Conscript-level finish, we are also going to paint the puttees at this stage. These colours are painted on using the thinned-down paint as detailed in Step 2 of the Conscript guide, but with the added need for slightly more drying time between colours.

Paints used

Area	Colour
Uniform	Vallejo 882 Middlestone
Skin	Vallejo 803 Brown Rose
Puttees	Vallejo 830 German Field Grey

Brush: Size 1.

Step 3

Once the figure is completely dry, dry-brush it using the techniques outlined in Chapter 1 (Tools of the Trade), and you will get the best results if you allow the colour to build up with several layers of dry-brushing as opposed to loading up the brush with too much paint. Although I suggest using a very pale sand-coloured paint, you could use white or ivory instead if you want a greater contrast.

Paints used

Area	Colour
Whole Figure	Vallejo 837 Pale Sand

Brush: Flat-headed, size ½.

Step 4

This stage is optional, however it will help to unify the different layers of colour on the figure's skin and uniform, and take away any highlights that might have ended up being harsher than intended with the previous step. As in Step 2, we will be thinning the paints down, however this time using more water, so that the paint is even thinner, at a ratio of about two parts water, to one part paint.

Unsurprisingly, this will be quite prone to running, so be careful how you apply it, but you want to use one thin layer over each of the relevant colours, and be very careful not to allow the paint to pool or build up or run. It's probably worth doing the skin and puttees first, then finishing the uniform once these other areas have dried, to prevent the paints contaminating one another, whilst also minimizing the amount of down time you have.

Area	Colour
Uniform	Vallejo 882 Middlestone
Skin	Vallejo 803 Brown Rose
Puttees	Vallejo 830 German Field Grey

Brush: Size 1.

Step 5

At this stage, all we need to do is paint the colours onto his equipment and remaining parts of his uniform. Again, we're using a black ink on the feathers of his helmet; the ink is also a little glossy, adding an extra level of detail and interest to the model. If you wish to, you can also add some Army Painter Dark Tone to the weapons, to make them a little darker and shade the wood and metal work, though, as ever, this is largely down to personal taste.

Area	Colour
Helmet	Vallejo 976 Buff
Feathers	Vallejo Game Colour 094 Black Ink
Webbing	Vallejo 896 Basalt Grey
Rifle stock	Vallejo 836 Mahogany Brown
Metal work	Vallejo 863 Gunmetal
Puttees	Vallejo 830 German Field Grey
Boots	Vallejo 862 Black Grey

Brush: Size 1.

Step 6

Now that our Bersaglieri is almost done, to add a bit more subtle depth and shading to him we're going to paint the whole figure with some Army Painter soft tone ink. This will serve two functions: firstly, shade the model; and secondly, as the name implies, it will pull all the colours on the figure together tonally. Simply paint this over the entire model in a thin layer, being mindful to not allow the tone to pool or flood the detail.

Paints used

Area	Colour
Whole figure	Army Painter Soft Tone

Brush: Size 1.

With Step 6 done, we have another Italian figure finished! This set of techniques leaves a lot open to interpretation and personal taste, so benefits from some experimentation. The use of heavily thinned paint works particularly well on figures sculpted with notably deep detail. Regular level finish complete!

ELITE LEVEL

Keeping with the theme of using thinned paints over a white base coat, this guide will draw some stages from both the Conscript and Regular finishes, and also use layered highlights rather than dry-brushing to detail and bring the model to life. So, as with the others, grab your primer and get painting.

Step 1

	Paints Used	

Area	Colour
Whole figure	White car primer

Brush: None.

Step 2

As at the regular level, we will be using thinned-down layers to put the base colours onto the uniform, skin and puttees, allowing the paint to dry over the primer in such a way that it creates some naturally highlighted and shaded clothing and skin.

Paints used

Area	Colour
Uniform	Vallejo 882 Middlestone
Skin	Vallejo 803 Brown Rose
Puttees	Vallejo 830 German Field Grey

Brush: Size 1.

Step 3

Nothing overly exciting in Step 3; all we are doing is laying down the foundation colours for the figure's equipment and weapons.

Area	Colour
Helmet	Vallejo 976 Buff
Feathers	Vallejo Game Colour 094 Black Ink
Webbing	Vallejo 896 Basalt Grey
Rifle stock	Vallejo 836 Mahogany Brown
Metal work	Vallejo 863 Gunmetal
Puttees	Vallejo 830 German Field Grey
Boots	Vallejo 862 Black Grey

Brush: Size 1.

Step 4

At this stage, we have a figure with their uniform and field gear nicely painted in, and ready for the highlighting to begin. As shown in Chapter 1 (Tools of the Trade), we'll be applying a layer of highlights to the uniform, skin, puttees and wood work of the rifle. You could use some light greys for the boots and webbing. However, as there are a few more steps to go, highlighting these parts of the figure isn't that necessary. Don't let this stop you experimenting though.

Area	Colour
Uniform	Vallejo 976 Buff
Skin	Vallejo 955 Flat Flesh
Puttees	Vallejo 886 Green Grey
Woodwork	Vallejo 981 Orange Brown

Brush: Size 1.

Step 5

With the initial layer of highlights in place, we can add a second layer. You may feel these aren't necessary, especially given the shading effects already in place, with the first layers of colour being applied over white. That said, I find the additional level of contrast adds in some extra character and wow factor to the model, especially once all the stages are finished. These are simply applied to the same areas of the figure as were highlighted in Step 4 but with the highlights more tightly placed on only the most prominent parts of the model.

Paints used

Area	Colour
Uniform	Vallejo 837 Pale Sand
Skin	Vallejo 815 Basic Skin Tone
Puttees	Vallejo 885 Pastel Green

Brush: Size 0.

Step 6

By now the figure will be starting to look nice. However, with some many techniques in place, there is a risk it could start to look a little messy, chalky or uncoordinated. We want to try to add some warmth back into the colours, as well as adding in some depth to the recesses, given such pale and bright colours already on the figure, and the shading tones should be chosen with this in mind. Using too dark a tone would run the risk of darkening the colours on the figure, and may overwhelm the effects already applied too.

Area	Colour
Helmet	Army Painter Soft Tone
Uniform	Army Painter Soft Tone
Webbing	Army Painter Soft Tone
Skin	Army Painter Flesh Tone
Boots	Army Painter Strong Tone
Woodwork	Army Painter Dark Tone
Metalwork	Army Painter Dark Tone

Brush: Size 1.

Step 7

In this final step, our Bersaglieri is finished off with some final spot highlights to the most raised, prominent parts of the figure. These are applied as with any other layered highlights, though they should be used sparingly, to prevent the figure appearing to be too pale or over highlighted.

Whilst I have listed different highlight colours for the uniform, flesh and puttees, if you wanted to try out giving the figure a more dusty, sun-worn look you could use a pale sand colour instead. This will serve to make it appear a little desaturated and bleached too, which can be quite an appealing, albeit quite stylized finish. As ever, never be afraid to try out ideas and colours that work for you.

Paints used

Area	Colour
Helmet	Vallejo 976 Buff
Uniform	Vallejo 837 Pale Sand
Webbing	Vallejo 896 Basalt Grey
Rifle stock	Vallejo 981 Orange Brown
Metal work	Vallejo 863 Gunmetal
Puttees	Vallejo 885 Pastel Green
Boots	Vallejo 862 Black Grey

Brush: Size 0.

With so many steps this is quite a complex method of painting. However, a squad of figures painted using this technique will look stunning; even when reserved to officers or vehicle commanders it gives you a pleasing chance to flex your painting muscles for the more important models in your collection. When spread over a full army, however, you can quickly learn some

short cuts and start to process models quicker than the process would suggest, though this does require a certain amount of dedication to get a gaming-sized force finished. Elite level finish complete!

The Italian army presents a few interesting challenges for the painter. With a wide range of tropical equipment issued, there is plenty of room to factor in differing shades of khaki and desert sand for their uniforms. Likewise, if you want to work in some more colours to figures dressed in steel helmets it is a simple matter to paint a few figures wearing those in grey for some more visual variety.

The presence of troops such as the colonial Askari, camouflaged uniformed paratroopers and, as painted in our guide, feather-wearing Bersaglieri, allows you to collect an interesting and varied array of models for your shelves, as well as creating a series of new modelling and hobby challenges for yourself as your collection grows.

Whilst the above steps have focussed on 28mm sized figures, with each guide being largely based around highly thinned paints and some controlled highlights, the painting guides can easily be translated to models of other size and styles. However, if you work with 15mm figures or smaller you can probably dispense with a few of the highlight stages quite comfortably.

5

Painting the
United States Army

With the entry of the United States into the Second
World War in December 1941, pressure from the Soviet
Union had been steadily increasing to open a second
front in Europe, to relieve pressure on the Eastern
Front. Initial American plans had called for the launch
of Operation Sledge Hammer in the latter half of 1942;
however, following British criticism of the plan, as well as

the raid on Dieppe demonstrating the sheer difficulty of assaulting a well-prepared opponent with an amphibious force, it was decided to direct their efforts into an expanded operation elsewhere.

By 1942 the seesaw battles in North Africa had seen both Axis and Allied forces alternating between positions of advantage, with neither force able to deliver a knockout blow. In order to free up Allied forces in Africa for further operations in the Mediterranean, it was deemed necessary to drive Axis forces from Africa, and then allow landings to occur in Sicily and Italy, appeasing the Soviets with a second front until further amphibious landings could occur in France in 1944.

Allied planners identified targets in Algeria, Morocco, and Tunisia in Vichy French North Africa as key targets for Operation Torch, with the aim being quickly to land forces and advance rapidly into Tunisia, cutting off Axis lines of supply and forcing the surrender of Army Group Africa.

Vichy forces were nominally neutral, however repeated clashes between British and Vichy French forces had somewhat soured diplomatic relations between the two nations. With the campaign against Axis targets in Tunisia intended to be as rapid as possible, steps were made to secure Vichy cooperation, and General Eisenhower of the US Army was placed as Commander-in-Chief of the allied ground forces, though Admiral Cunningham of the Royal Navy was in command of Naval operations. American forces were selected to be the assault troops as these were deemed likely to lead to better public relations with Vichy forces, though several British Brigades also took part in the landings. The troops landing were ordered not to fire unless fired upon and, although several Vichy coastal batteries did engage and were swiftly overcome, the former Vichy forces eventually formed a part of the Free French forces in Africa.

Progressing into Tunisia from their Algerian jump off points, allied forces sought to swiftly reach the port of Tunis before Axis forces could be reinforced and entrenched too strongly. The inexperienced American forces met one of their toughest tests at the Battle of Kasserine Pass, when a German and Italian counteroffensive struck at one of the few navigable passes through the Atlas Mountains that border Tunisia and Algeria.

Initially, Rommel's attack was very successful, sweeping the still-green American forces and their French allies from the pass; though the resistance the Allies provided proved to be greater than the Axis forces had anticipated, they still suffered massive losses in men and matériel. As the Axis attack ground on, however, increasingly stubborn resistance, as well as sustained artillery fire, eventually drove them to halt, before being ordered to withdraw back to their initial start locations.

US forces at Kasserine Pass were hampered by inflexible command and control doctrines, as well as an inability to respond to tactically fluid situations. The M3 Stuart and M3 Lee tanks also proved inferior in stand-up fights with the latest German armour designs, and there had been limited uptake of knowledge learned by British and Commonwealth forces in fighting Axis doctrine.

From this, whilst the Axis and especially German high command would be somewhat scornful of American capabilities, the American forces quickly assimilated their hard-won tactical knowledge, and implemented means to have greater and more rapid artillery and air support available, as well as giving commanders more discretion to adopt to changing situations. As a result of this, US forces would go on to give good accounts of themselves wherever they fought for the rest of the war.

The Army of the United States' uniform was intended to consist of a series of layers of clothing, with an outer layer comprising of light khaki-coloured waist-length M1941 'Parsons' field jacket, and olive brown-coloured wool trousers, to which was added khaki webbing and an olive drab helmet. This uniform would go on to be the iconic appearance of the American soldier in the Second World War, though it would eventually be replaced by more modern equipment.

Due to the layered system of clothing, as well as much of the American involvement in the North African campaign taking place during the winter months, a specific tropical uniform such as that used by the other belligerents was not issued. That said, American troops did have a light-weight olive grey Herringbone uniform that was also worn, and both of these uniforms would appear in Sicily, Italy, Normandy and the Far East.

Today, we will be painting a 28mm plastic figure from the Warlord Games range, and this is assembled using the skills covered in Chapter 2 (Boot Camp). As ever, the skills and techniques used here can apply to any figure you may have, and you can feel free to apply any of the guides for other nationalities here by simply using the colours listed below with those processes.

CONSCRIPT LEVEL

Our plan for this figure is to come up with a fairly muted scheme, though one that still has some nice contrasts between highlight and shade, with the least amount of time and work. To do this, we will simply be starting with some layers of shading inks, and applying this over a primer before picking out the details. First up though, give your figure a nice, even coat of grey primer.

Step 1

Paints used

Area	Colour
Whole figure	Grey car primer

Brush: None.

Step 2

In this stage, we are going to paint the main areas of the figure's uniform. To do so, you can either use a pre-mixed shading tone, such as those created by Vallejo or Army

Painter (amongst others), or make your own as covered in Chapter 1 (Tools of the Trade). We'll be using two at this stage: an olive green colour for the figure's jacket, webbing and gaiters; and a dark brown for the figure's trousers.

Apply this as evenly as you can to the figure and don't worry if the colour seems thin, this is fine as you can go over a few layers to get a level of colour density you prefer. Two or three layers are infinitely preferable to one heavy one, though it's important to allow the preceding layer at least an hour to dry.

Don't worry about the areas of skin, shoes, helmet or weapons at this stage, we'll come to those later.

Area	Colour
Jacket, webbing, gaiters	Army Painter Military Shader
Trousers	Army Painter Strong Tone.

Brush: Size 1.

Step 3

Now we pick out the areas of detail on the figure. With so much of the model already shaded, you can either use these to apply a single, solid colour to their respective areas, or allow some of the shade areas to remain in the recesses by being a little more careful and precise with your application of paint. Both option works, and it's entirely down to personal preference. For the figure in the photos, I have allowed some of the shade colours to remain on the webbing and weapon.

For the areas of skin, simply apply a neat layer or two as needed of flat flesh for this stage.

Paints used

Area	Colour
Skin	Vallejo 955 Flat Flesh
Helmet	Vallejo 887 Brown Violet
Webbing and gaiters	Vallejo 882 Middlestone
Rifle stock	Vallejo 836 Mahogany Brown
Metal work	Vallejo 863 Gunmetal
Boots	Vallejo 836 Mahogany Brown

Brush: Size 1.

Step 4

The figure is almost finished, and would be perfectly useable as is; however, if you want to really make it pop without much extra effort, simply apply a dark wash or shade to the figure's weapon, and a flesh shading wash to the areas of skin, and you're done!

Area	Colour
Skin	Army Painter Flesh Tone
Weapon	Army Painter Dark Tone.
Webbing, boots and helmet	Army Painter Soft Tone

Paints used

Brush: Size 1.

Conscript stage ready! As with all the Conscript-level finishes, I've tried to present a set of techniques, the above four steps will allow you to produce a very simple

but effective figure, and whilst it works for a single figure, it is also ideally suited to mass production or batch painting of models as well.

REGULAR LEVEL

With the Regular level of finish we will be using many of the same principles as covered in the Conscript level, however there will be some extra refinements, and the overall goal is, with the addition of a few extra simple steps, to create something notably more detailed without a massive time investment or requirement for too much precision.

In Step 1, we will actually be applying two stages of priming. The first, as ever, is to ensure an even coverage of grey over the whole model. The second part of this process is a little different, and we are going to use the white to create some instant shading and contrast.

This is quite a simple process once you are familiar with it, but can be a little tricky at first. Once the grey has become at least touch dry, spray some white primer onto the figure holding the can at approximately a 45-degree angle. Hold the can at a distance that allows the paint to land on the most prominent areas, whilst retaining some of the grey in the recesses and lower parts of the model. All spray cans are different, though I'd recommend holding the can at around 20-30cm from the figure. As with any new technique, it's always best to do a practice run on some spare models before committing to your treasured new project.

Step 1

Area	Colour
Whole figure	Grey car primer
Whole figure	White car primer

Step 2

This step is largely identical to that in the Conscript level. However, as we are now working over white, you may need a few more layers of washes to prevent the model appearing too pale. Also, with the white base it is even more important to ensure the paint does not pool or run, so when loading your brush it's definitely a case of less is more at this step!

Paints used

Area	Colour
Jacket, webbing gaiters	Army Painter Military Shader
Trousers	Army Painter Strong Tone.

Brush: Size 1.

Step 3

Again, as with the conscript step, we are simply blocking colours into the model, though we won't be painting the figure's weapon or helmet at this stage, as we don't want the following dry-brush to affect those areas. This is purely personal preference, however, and you may still block them in now if you so wish.

Area	Colour
Skin	Vallejo 955 Flat Flesh
Webbing and gaiters	Vallejo 882 Middlestone
Boots	Vallejo 836 Mahogany Brown

Step 4

Whilst our model has a good amount of contrast in place already, a very light dry brushing of pale sand will really give him some character and help to pull the almost-finished figure together. It's optional, but I recommend it. This step will also serve to highlight the flesh areas too.

Paints used

Area	Colour
Whole Figure	Vallejo 837 Pale Sand

Brush: Flat-headed, size ½.

Step 5

It's now time to add in the final tidying details, so block in the colours on the model's weapons and helmet; also, any bayonets, ammunition boxes, grenades and entrenching tool handles should be picked out with the same colour as the helmet.

Area	Colour
Helmet	Vallejo 887 Brown Violet
Rifle stock	Vallejo 836 Mahogany Brown
Metal work	Vallejo 863 Gunmetal

Brush: Size 1.

Step 6

The final stage is to add a few last washes to the model. On my example I have just applied a wash to the weapon and skin areas of the figure. If you feel the dry-brush created too much contrast, or maybe you applied the paint a little too heavily, you can go back and repeat Step 2 as well to tone the brightness down somewhat.

Area	Colour
Skin	Army Painter Flesh Tone
Weapon	Army Painter Dark Tone.
Webbing, boots and helmet	Army Painter Soft Tone

Brush: Size 1.

Whilst most of the techniques for this Regular-level finish are fairly similar to those of the Conscript, the initial highlighting provided with the white priming stage, as well as the dry-brushing, give a very different look to the figure. Key to this finish is practice as, though initially it may appear daunting, it can give a very quick but also a very good looking army. It is also particularly well suited to small-scale figures, especially those sized 15mm and smaller. Regular-level finish complete!

ELITE LEVEL

For our Elite level of finish we will be working over a white base, and then again using a series of washes to get the initial layers of colour down, before using the layering technique to paint in both highlights and also areas of shade. This particular finish is quite heavily reliant on brush control, so it is even more important than usual to use a high-quality brush for the layering. First up, we just have to prime the figure with a nice and even coat of white.

Step 1

Paints Used

Area	Colour
Whole figure	White car primer

Brush: None.

Step 2

As with both previous levels, we are going to apply some washes to the model to allow the colour to begin shading itself. As we are working over pure white, this may well require three to four coats to get a good and opaque colour; the trick is to apply the paint neat enough for it to pool in the recesses, without flooding the model too. Then repeat as many times as necessary to get a level of colour density that you like.

I'd suggest also applying the strong tone to the figure's weapons, skin, boots and helmet, though it's not entirely necessary. By applying the wash you will, however, give a nice already shaded base to work up from when you come to painting in those areas with their block colours later.

Area	Colour
Jacket, webbing gaiters	Army Painter Military Shader
Trousers; optionally: helmet, boots, weapon and skin.	Army Painter Strong Tone.

Brush: Size 1.

Step 3

In Step 3 we start to block in the colours that we will be adding the layered highlights to later on. If you added the optional shades from Step 2 to the figure, ensure you only apply the colours in this stage to the raised parts of the model, and allow the shadows to remain visible. This is going to be time consuming, but well worth it in the end.

When painting the face and hands, cover most of the area but leave areas around the chin strap, eyes, below the nose and between the lips and fingers with your darker layer still visible.

Area	Colour
Skin	Vallejo 850 Medium Flesh Tone
Helmet	Vallejo 887 Brown Violet
Webbing and gaiters	Vallejo 882 Middlestone
Rifle stock	Vallejo 836 Mahogany Brown
Metal work	Vallejo 863 Gunmetal
Boots	Vallejo 836 Mahogany Brown

Brush: Size 1.

Step 4

With this step, we are going to use the layering technique to apply some extra shadow to the figure. This paint should be thinned to around the consistency of milk, and you should use whichever brush you have that provides you the most control and accuracy. I've suggested a size 0, though really any brush you have that fulfils these criteria works.

Take a moment to look at the figure and see where the light naturally falls to create shadow; this is likely to be the recesses of the face, deep creases in clothing, as well as between the legs and the underside of the arms. Simply paint into the very darkest areas. With your paint suitably thinned, this should naturally blend and flow into the shadow.

I advise against applying this to every shadow on the model, as there is a risk it will create too much contrast.

Paints used

Area	Colour
Skin	Vallejo 836 Mahogany Brown
Webbing and gaiters	Vallejo 889 Olive Drab
Trousers and jacket	Vallejo 889 Olive Drab

Brush: Size 0.

Step 5

In contrast to the previous step's application of deep shade, in this step we will apply a first step of highlights, again using paint thinned down to the consistency roughly of milk.

This time, we will be applying the paint to the areas of the figure that naturally catch the light, such as tops of shoulders and arms, prominent clothing folds, fingers, tops of webbing, tips of noses, cheeks, and so on.

Paints used

Area	Colour
Jacket	Vallejo 987 Medium Grey
Trousers	Vallejo 825 German Camo Beige Brown
Skin	Vallejo 955 Flat Flesh
Webbing and gaiters	Vallejo 976 Buff
Boots	Vallejo 818 Red Leather
Weapon stock	Vallejo 818 Red Leather

Brush: Size 0.

Step 6

Before we finish off the Elite-level finish with a final highlight, we will add a glaze to the model using a few selected tones. These are applied similarly to a wash, however we don't want them to discolour the work we have already applied so should instead be applied sparingly. The goal is for these to bring our work so far together, as well as smoothing out the different layers that have been building up on the model.

Area	Colour
Helmet	Army Painter Soft Tone
Uniform	Army Painter Soft Tone
Webbing	Army Painter Soft Tone
Skin	Army Painter Flesh Tone
Boots	Army Painter Strong Tone
Weaponry	Army Painter Dark Tone

Brush: Size 1.

Step 7

At last we are nearly done! In this step we will add some final highlights. Again, look to apply these to only the most very prominent areas of the figure. With this stage be sparing in your highlights, as the figure could otherwise end up looking somewhat washed out. Do a few, see how it looks, then if you think the model needs a few more highlights it's a simple matter of slowly adding them until you are satisfied.

Paints used

Area	Colour
Jacket	Vallejo 987 Medium Grey
Webbing	Vallejo 976 Buff
Trousers	Vallejo 987 Medium Grey
Boots	Vallejo 818 Red Leather
Skin	Vallejo 815 Basic Skin Tone
Helmet	Vallejo 887 Brown Violet

Brush: Size 0.

With that, the figure is done! Obviously this is a very labour-intensive and protracted process, however the finished model looks striking too. Whether this is worth the extra amount of time and effort required is entirely up to you to decide; personally, however, I find once you have a squad or two painted like this the urge to see a completed force is enough to get me through the rest of the project. Elite-level finish complete!

6

Painting the German Army

Like many European countries, prior to the end of the First World War Germany had maintained a small empire across Africa. However, with Germany's defeat and the signing of the Treaty of Versailles, this was disbanded and shared out to the various victorious allied powers.

With the rise of the Nazi party and Hitler coming into power in 1933, a rearmed Germany once more advanced across Europe, and by mid-1940 most of continental Europe was under Axis control. From this

position, German high command was begging to execute their invasion of Russia, scheduled for early summer in 1941. Simultaneous with Germany's conquest of Europe, their Italian allies had been expanding their empire across the Balkans and northern Africa. However, unexpected reversals of fortune had seen the Italians stalled in both theatres, and German forces earmarked for the invasion of Russia were directed to assist the Italians.

Arriving in Libya in February 1941 with the German 5th Light Division, Generalleutnant Erwin Rommel swiftly went onto the offensive. In an aggressive campaign, Axis forces quickly retook ground from the British and Commonwealth forces, before being driven back into Tunisia following General Auchinleck's counterattack.

Despite this setback, the German and Italian forces were steadily reinforced with further divisions until in 1943 there were four German divisions in North Africa, as well as ten Italian. Collectively, the German forces would come to be known as the Deutsches Afrika Korps. Thus reinforced, Axis forces began a new offensive in early 1942. From this point on, the war in the desert would swing backwards and forwards between Axis and Allied attacks and counterattacks, until the 1943 landings in Tunisia sounded the death knell for the Axis forces in Afrika.

With the urgent need for German troops to deploy to Africa, a tropical uniform was swiftly devised that retained a similar cut to the M40 woollen uniform worn in Europe but was manufactured in a light olive green-coloured material. When first introduced, colour variation ranged from dark green to a sand colour, though by 1941 the colours had been standardized. Alongside the light olive tropical uniform, a brown woollen tropical great coat was also introduced, as was a tropical cap of similar style to the peaked cap worn by German mountain troops, and similar in style to a baseball cap.

With such a comparatively dark-coloured uniform, sun bleaching was fairly rapid, and the actual colour of Afrika Korps uniforms could vary quite significantly, with clothing appearing almost white after continued exposure to the harsh desert conditions.

The Luftwaffe was issued a sand-coloured uniform, with a different cut and baggier trousers, though it still had similar headwear and four-pocket tunic to the army, again in sand colour. Despite orders to the contrary, the supply situation that plagued the Afrika Korps carried over into their uniforms as well, and Luftwaffe, Italian and captured Allied clothing can be seen being worn by the forces from the Heer (German Army), as well.

Camouflage clothing was limited, largely being confined to the jump smocks of the Fallschirmjäger (Paratroopers), and this was in the standard Luftwaffe splinter pattern. I'll look more into painting camouflage in a later section of the book.

Apart from uniform, German forces were also issued with specifically designed tropical webbing and footwear. The webbing was formed from a khaki canvas belt, to which were attached shoulder straps, ammunition pouches, holsters, bread bags, water bottles and entrenching tools, as well a host of other equipment. Rifle ammunition pouches tended to be a brown or black leather, whilst the larger rectangular ones for the MP40 submachine gun were in the same khaki material as the rest of the webbing.

Boots were made from a red-brown leather, with green canvas upper parts to them, and were issued as both a short ankle boot, and longer calf-length item. Pith helmets were issued, and came in a pale khaki colour, though steel helmets were common from late 1941, especially in combat. These, along with the other metal items of field equipment, were generally painted in the field with a variety of tones of sand or ochre paint, and hessian helmet covers were also somewhat common.

Our Afrika Korps soldier is going to be a 20mm single-piece metal figure from The Plastic Soldier Company, and he will be wearing items of clothing representing different levels of weathering and fading. As with all of these guides, the techniques translate across figure scales and sizes, so can be used for larger 28mm or smaller 15mm models, or any other size you happen to be working with.

CONSCRIPT LEVEL

With our Afrika Korp figure cleaned and prepped, we will start by priming him using a matt black automotive primer. This will ensure that the paint surface is up to the rigours of table-top handling, as well as bonding well to the metal of the figure.

This figure will be wearing a darker olive tunic, and a set of paler, almost khaki trousers, indicating that he has a replacement or new tunic. However, either of the colours used here can be used interchangeably on either the caps, tunics or trousers that your Afrika Korps figures wear, and may also be used to give a figure with any and all items in a matching, uniform colour.

Step 1

Paints used

Area	Colour
Whole figure	Black car primer

Brush: None

Step 2

With our primer dry, we will start to block in some of the colours of the figure's clothing, skin and uniform. You'll need to be fairly neat at this stage, however it's not massively critical if you have a few areas of errant paint. We aren't going to pick out things like the figure's boots or weapons now, as we don't want those to receive any dry-brushing in the next stage.

Paints used

Area	Colour
Uniform Tunic	Vallejo 890 Refractive Green
Uniform Trousers	Vallejo 882 Middlestone
Skin	Vallejo 803 Brown Rose
Webbing	Vallejo 976 Buff
Helmet and metal items of field gear	Vallejo 824 German Camouflage Orange Ochre

Brush: Size 1

Step 3

For our highlights, the whole figure, including the flesh and webbing, is going to be dry-brushed (as described in Chapter 1: Tools of the Trade), with some Pale Sand paint. This will serve a twofold purpose: first, it will highlight the model (unsurprisingly); and secondly, it will serve to unify all the differently coloured areas, and give a hint of a dusty feel to the figure too. Remember to keep your brush very dry, and allow the paint to slowly build up as opposed to going in with a wet or loaded brush.

Paints Used	

Area	Colour
Whole figure	Vallejo 837 Pale Sand

Brush: Size ½, flat-headed

Step 4

With this step, all we are doing is picking the details not covered at the previous stage. These include the figures weapons, boots and ammunition pouches if he is carrying a rifle, or holster and tool pouch if a machine gunner. Remember, that the rifle pouches can be either brown or black leather, machine gun tool box and holsters are also black leather, whilst the pouches for the MP40 are the same colour as the rest of the figure's webbing. If you wish, you can put a layer of army painter dark tone over the metallic parts of a figures weapons.

This particular figure is wearing goggles, and I've painted the strap for these with red leather, and the lenses with blue ink.

Area	Colour
Rifle stock, water bottle, entrenching tool haft	Vallejo 836 Mahogany Brown
Metalwork	Vallejo 863 Gunmetal
Ammunition pouches, if relevant.	Vallejo Vallejo 818 Red Leather or Vallejo 995 German Grey
Boots	Vallejo 818 Red Leather, and 823 Luftwaffe Camouflage Green

And with that, our first recruit for the Afrika Korps is completed! As with all the Conscript-level finishes, it is designed to give you a quick and pleasing force for gaming as soon as possible, with minimal investment of time. A few tweaks such as the use of dark tone or a black wash on the metal pieces will really make the model stand out,

but happily this is something that you can always return to and add to the figure at a later stage should you wish too. Conscript level ready!

REGULAR LEVEL

Step 1

With the Regular-level finish, we are going to be letting the black primer do some shading work for us as well as simply giving a solid base to work up from. This figure is going to be painted using stages of layered highlights, and each step of the painting guide will detail the colours I've used for the first and second levels of highlights; however, if you wished to spend an evening painting say all the olive green items of clothing in a section you can of course mix and match sequences to suit your own personal tastes.

Paints Used

Area	Colour
Whole figure	Black car primer

Brush: None

Step 2

Now that our figure has a black base for us to work up from, we can start to paint in the first layers of colours. The use of the black primer will probably darken down the colours a little more than they might normally appear. However, this fits well with the overall finished effect we will be working towards. If you wish, you can leave some of the black showing in the darkest recesses of clothing and between webbing and uniform, however I find this is too stark a contrast for my tastes, and I tend to simply block all my colours in on a model.

Paints Used

Area	Colour
Uniform Tunic	Vallejo 890 Refractive Green
Uniform Trousers	Vallejo 882 Middlestone
Skin	Vallejo 803 Brown Rose
Webbing	Vallejo 976 Buff
Helmet and metal items of field gear	Vallejo 824 German Camouflage Orange Ochre
Rifle stock, water bottle, entrenching tool haft	Vallejo 836 Mahogany Brown
Metalwork	Vallejo 863 Gunmetal
Ammunition pouches, if relevant.	Vallejo 818 Red Leather or Vallejo 995 German Grey
Boots	Vallejo 818 Red Leather, and 823 Luftwaffe Camouflage Green

Brush: Size 1

Step 3

To start adding depth and volume to our model, we will now start to layer on some highlights. We will ultimately add two layers of these, however this step will detail the first of my colour choices for the highlights. Contrast between highlights is very subjective, and you may well have your own preferences or styles you wish to use. Please feel free to do so, and to experiment as well and create your own combinations of light and shade.

You will also note that some areas I have chosen not to highlight, again, this is personal choice with the focus being to balance speed of completion with detail.

Area	Colour
Uniform Tunic	Vallejo 882 Middlestone
Uniform Trousers	Vallejo 976 Buff
Skin	Vallejo 955 Flat Flesh
Webbing	Vallejo 837 Pale Sand
Helmet	Vallejo 976 Buff
Rifle stock, water bottle, entrenching tool haft	Vallejo 818 Red Leather
Metalwork	None
Ammunition pouches, if relevant.	None
Boots	None

Brush: Size 0

Step 4

Following in from Step 3, we will add the final detail highlights to the figure. At this stage we will also add a dark wash to the metal parts of the figure to give them a more realistic look.

The contrast between some of these highlights and previous layers may seem quite stark, so keeping your paint well thinned, as well as a little practice, may be needed to gain the best results, but will give you a very striking figure. As with the previous stage, some areas will not be getting a highlight, though feel free to add your own if you wish.

Paints Used

Area	Colour
Uniform Tunic	Vallejo 976 Buff
Uniform Trousers	Vallejo 837 Pale Sand
Skin	Vallejo 815 Basic Skin Tone
Webbing	Optional: White
Helmet	None
Rifle stock, water bottle, entrenching tool haft	None
Metalwork	Black wash or Army Painter Dark Tone
Ammunition pouches, if relevant.	None
Boots	None

Brush Size 0

Through these stages you will probably have noticed that I am using many of the same paints for different levels of highlight and areas of the figure. This is firstly to keep costs down, but also because it serves to help tie all the colours on a model together, and help make

his clothing and equipment appear as if it belongs on the same individual. As you work through a force, especially one where there is some variety in clothing colours such as with an Afrika Korps army, this can be an important trick in making quite disparate and rag-tag figures appear as if they still belong together. Regular level finish complete!

ELITE LEVEL

Step 1

In many ways the Regular and Elite levels of the Afrika Korps painting guide are very similar, and the initial stages are largely the same. However, where they differ is in the use of shading inks and final layers of highlights. As a result, this is a prime example of a technique you can bring back into your figures if you were willing to add some extra detail further down the line after you had initially finished them

Paints Used

Area	Colour
Whole figure	Black car primer

Brush: None

Step 2

Here again, we are simply blocking in the basic colours of the figure's uniform. One redeeming quality of this technique is that we can afford to be a little rougher with neatness, as the layers of highlights and shading washes will cover some sins, and allow us to work over others. Certainly has to be some reward to all this extra work!

Paints Used

Area	Colour
Uniform Tunic	Vallejo 890 Refractive Green
Uniform Trousers	Vallejo 882 Middlestone
Skin	Vallejo 803 Brown Rose
Webbing	Vallejo 976 Buff
Helmet and metal items of field gear	Vallejo 824 German Camouflage Orange Ochre
Rifle stock, water bottle, entrenching tool haft	Vallejo 836 Mahogany Brown
Metalwork	Vallejo 863 Gunmetal
Ammunition pouches, if relevant.	Vallejo Vallejo 818 Red Leather or Vallejo 995 German Grey
Boots	Vallejo 818 Red Leather, and 823 Luftwaffe Camouflage Green

Brush: Size 1

Step 3

First highlights go down. It may seem counter-intuitive to put highlights on to a figure before it receives a shading wash; however, having several layers of colour applied before the washes, gives a much deeper and richer feel to the colours and overall figure.

Area	Colour
Uniform Tunic	Vallejo 882 Middlestone
Uniform Trousers	Vallejo 976 Buff
Skin	Vallejo 955 Flat Flesh

Area	Colour
Webbing	Vallejo 837 Pale Sand
Helmet	Vallejo 976 Buff
Rifle stock, water bottle, entrenching tool haft	Vallejo 818 Red Leather
Metalwork	None
Ammunition pouches, if relevant.	None
Boots	None

Brush Size 0

Step 4

Yup, more highlights. You can dispense with these if you wish; however, I like to add them as it creates a smoother graduation between the final colours on the figure when it is completed. If you choose not to add this layer though, you may lose a little of the subtlety of the finish, but will have a figure that probably 'pops' a little more at gaming distances especially. Ultimately it comes down to personal taste.

Area	Colour
Uniform Tunic	Vallejo 976 Buff
Uniform Trousers	Vallejo 837 Pale Sand
Skin	Vallejo 815 Basic Skin Tone
Webbing	Optional:- White
Helmet	None
Rifle stock, water bottle, entrenching tool haft	None
Metalwork	Black wash or Army Painter Dark Tone
Ammunition pouches, if relevant.	None
Boots	None

Step 5

This is where the finish starts to differ from the Regular level, and everything from this point onwards is optional, and again largely boils down to personal taste and how much work you want to invest into a figure.

We will be applying shade to the figure, in this instance I'm using the Army Painter tones, however there are a great many pre-mixed washes out on the market, and any soft brown, black, olive green and flesh-coloured washes can be used if you wish, depending what you have access too.

You can also use this step to add an extra layer of shade to the metalwork on the figure's weapons if you want to dull them down further.

Area	Colour
Uniform Tunic	Army Painter Military Shader
Uniform Trousers	Army Painter Soft Tone
Skin	Army Painter Flesh Tone
Webbing	Army Painter Soft Tone
Helmet	Army Painter Soft Tone
Rifle stock, water bottle, entrenching tool haft	Army Painter Strong Tone
Metalwork (optional)	Black wash or Army Painter Dark Tone
Ammunition pouches, if relevant.	Army Painter Strong Tone
Boots	Army Painter Soft Tone

Brush: Size 1

Step 6

With this last step we bring in the final highlights. These are painted on smaller and tighter than those in Step 4, and are applied using the same colours as the previous brightest colour for that area before the washes were applied.

The reason for this, is that you will be creating a pleasing contrast with the colours that are already on the figure, without adding a huge jump between the previous highlight in tone. This all serves to make a more natural, softer and realistic finish to the figure, and also means you do not need any extra paints either!

With this last set of highlights added, our figure is done! This process has lots of stages, but as stated can be applied at a later date to a model painted using our Regular level of finish, or alternatively can be used as part of a production line, which can be hard work, but is also hugely rewarding when you are presented with a full squad of nicely finished figures.

Area	Colour
Uniform Tunic	Vallejo 976 Buff
Uniform Trousers	Vallejo 837 Pale Sand
Skin	Vallejo 815 Basic Skin Tone
Webbing	Optional:- White
Helmet	Vallejo 976 Buff
Rifle stock, water bottle, entrenching tool haft	Vallejo 818 Red Leather
Metalwork	Black wash or Army Painter Dark Tone
Ammunition pouches, if relevant.	Vallejo 818 Red Leather or Vallejo 995 German Grey
Boots	Vallejo 818 Red Leather, and 823 Luftwaffe Camouflage Green

Elite-level finish complete!

Painting an Afrika Korps force can be a phenomenally rewarding experience. Whilst initially they appear to be very uniform with the olive green uniform and sand helmets and field gear, the reality of fading and different equipment issues actually leads you into a fairly wide range of colour combinations that can give you a very interesting looking army that still is part of a uniform force.

Simply using the colours listed in this guide, you can create a varied looking force; however, if you were to branch out and use some of the other colour combinations in guides in this book you could have a very varied force indeed, though I would caution to keep at least some of the same paint combinations on each figure in the force, otherwise you run the risk of them looking too rag tag, and no longer like a unified fighting force.

7

Camouflage Uniforms

Disruptive camouflage was rarely seen in the desert campaign. The most frequent users were the German Paratroopers who arrived in the latter part of the campaign. If we take into account the Sicilian and Italian campaign, however, disruptive camouflage garments become far more common. For today though, I'll be focussing on the most prevalent pattern in North Africa.

The German airborne forces, the Fallschirmjäger, had spearheaded the Blitzkrieg across Europe in 1940, launching daring airborne operations to secure key strategic objectives. This culminated in 1941 with the invasion of the island of Crete, which, though ultimately successful, also lead to huge casualties in the Fallschirmjäger, and from that point on they spent most of the war operating as elite infantry.

First arriving in North Africa in 1942, the Fallschirmjäger deployed to this theatre lived up to their reputation as tough troops, fighting right up to the surrender in Tunisia, and beyond the conclusion of the African campaigns, with Fallschirmjäger fighting on all fronts through to the end of the war.

In terms of uniform, the Fallschirmjäger in Tunisia wore sand-coloured trousers and tunic, with a distinctive jump smock typically being worn over this. This smock could be either an earlier, step-in pattern garment that looks like a short boiler suit or onesie. This was issued first in a light olive colour, similar to the green uniform of our Afrika Korps guide, and later in splinter-pattern camouflage. Also worn was a later-pattern jump smock that resembles a knee-length coat. This was also issued in splinter-pattern camouflage, and this is what we will be painting today.

When painting camouflage, one has to exaggerate the colours used on the figure when compared to the historical counterpart, as when using the original colours on a small figure, they tend to merge into a dull, murky mess, especially at the distances from which we tend to be looking at our figures on the gaming table. With this in mind, during this guide I'll be leaving out the Regular level paint job, as we can achieve a pleasing camouflage pattern at the Conscript level, without creating extra work for ourselves. To save space, and avoid repetition, I'll be drawing colours for the uniform from the Italian guide, and for the webbing and equipment from the Afrika Korp guide, and will instead concentrate purely on how to do the camouflage. The figure used is a Perry Miniatures 28mm metal Fallschirmjäger.

As both the Conscript and Elite level guides start off with the same first three steps, when it comes to the Elite level guide I'll start straight off from step 4.

CONSCRIPT LEVEL

Step 1

As the figure will have some fairly complex colouring applied and be quite busy in appearance, we'll be priming him with a nice neutral grey as a base to work up from.

Paints Used

Area	Colour
Whole figure	Grey car primer

Step 2

Now, we'll paint in the first colour to be used on the smock. My preference when painting camouflage is to follow a logical sequence. Start with the most prevalent colour of the pattern, and work through them in order of frequency until the pattern is in place. At this stage we can also start to block in the basic colours of the rest of the figures uniform and equipment too. If your figure is wearing a helmet cover, paint this now too.

For splinter pattern, I like to start with the brown first, and simply paint each of the disruptive colours with small interconnected squares and triangles.

Paints used

Area	Colour
Jump smock, helmet cover too if worn.	Vallejo 885 Pastel Green

Brush: Size 1, round

Step 3

Time now to apply the disruptive pattern. With splinter-pattern camouflage, this looks terrifyingly complex, but when broken down is relatively simple. First, start by painting a series of jagged, dark brown strips over around half the surface area of the figure, ensuring you leave plenty of the base colour applied in Step 2 visible.

Once this is dry, repeat the process, applying the darker green to around a third of the figure, and ensuring that this green is attached to a part of the brown pattern, and that's all there is too it.

Paints used

Area	Colour
Jump smock, helmet cover too if worn. Brown pattern	Vallejo 983 Flat earth
Jump smock, helmet cover too if worn. Green pattern	Vallejo 823 Luftwaffe green

Brush: Size 0 round

Step 4

To finish off the camouflage, we're going to give the model a very light and subtle dry-brush, using Pale Sand. From this point on you can go on and finish the rest of the figure using whatever techniques you chose.

Paints Used

Area	Colour
Jump smock; helmet cover too, if worn.	Vallejo 837 Pale Sand

Brush: Size ½, flat

If you wanted to spend a little more time you could use a well-thinned Pale Sand and paint on some layered

highlights instead, however this is entirely down to personal preference, and the time constraints that you are working to.

ELITE LEVEL

As mentioned above, we use the first three steps from the Conscript level to lay down the basic colours, and to save repeating those now I'll begin at Step 4.

Step 4

As our camouflage pattern is starting to take shape, we can now start to bring it to life. This is a relatively simple step, but one that does require a steady hand and some attention to detail as well. We will be applying a layered highlight to each of the camouflage colours. Instead of highlight the entire crease or edge of clothing, paint the highlight onto the raised part of that pattern. It's a lot of work, but worth it!

Paints used

Area	Colour
Jump smock, helmet cover too if worn. Pale green base	Vallejo 971 Green Grey
Jump smock, helmet cover too if worn. Brown pattern	Vallejo825 German Camouflage pale brown
Jump smock, helmet cover too if worn. Green pattern	Vallejo 850 Medium olive.

Brush: Size 0, round

Step 5

Nearly there! At the moment the camouflage may be starting to look a little like it's lost some of its pattern, or a little too contrasting and unnatural. To bring everything back, we'll apply a light brown glaze to the figure. I'm going to use Army Painter Soft Tone, but you can mix your own or use another readymade product if you prefer. Simply glaze over the entire figure's jump smock.

Paints Used

Area	Colour
Jump smock, helmet cover too if worn.	Army Painter Soft Tone

Brush: Size 1 round

Step 6

To finish the figure, we are just going to apply some selective spot highlights of Pale Sand to the most prominent highlights using the layering method, and painting the highlights onto only the most prominent parts of the figure using some well thinned Pale Sand. With that, our Fallschirmjäger is complete!

Paints Used

Area	Colour
Jump smock, helmet cover too if worn.	Vallejo 837 Pale Sand

Brush: Size 0, round

With this guide, hopefully I've managed to simplify painting Fallschirmjäger camouflage smocks and still give a pleasing finish, both at a quick and efficient table level, and also as a more detailed finish too. Whilst the real splinter pattern features some very subtle rain streaks to help break up the outline of the pattern, I've decided to leave these out, as the effect of the figure's size would render these largely invisible anyway, though you could add them with a dark blue paint and very fine brush if you wish, adding a series of fine vertical stripes to the figure. I generally choose not to add them however, as I feel it detracts from the general impression of the camouflage.

8

Basing

By now we've looked at tools, we've assembled and painted our figures, and they are starting to look mighty smart indeed. Whilst everyone loves a beautifully painted platoon/company/battalion/army… the one thing that really does draw a force together and make it appear as a fighting force operating as one, is the basing. Put simply, basing a figure is to apply a textured finish to the model's stand, appropriate to the figure's setting or environment, paint it, and then apply a few details such as rocks or foliage for interest.

Whilst finishing the base is an easy stage to overlook or ignore, in my opinion it is probably the single most critical step of the entire process of painting a figure, as the base serves to frame the model, and is also the first thing you usually see, especially at a distance. A well-finished base can elevate a poor to moderate paint job, and conversely can detract from an otherwise-nicely painted figure.

A figure's base tells a story of where it is fighting, and, especially for the likes of weapon teams, if you choose to base the crew on one large base it can create a fantastically dynamic centrepiece of your force.

With any basing, it's important to keep it fairly subtle, so as not to overwhelm the model. An example of overwhelming basing could be a single figure hidden in amongst a pile of bushes, or in a pile of rubble, quite dramatic, but does also render it hard to actually see the model.

On the table top it can be a little difficult sometimes to discern where our squad leaders, machine gunners, and other specialists are lurking. Other times, when two sections are next to one another, it's quite possible for both units to get confused and difficult to determine which is which. This is where our basing comes in handy again.

A trick I like to use with my collection, is to use the same background on each base, so sand in the case of desert forces, and then mark out individual units with a subtle detail, so one squad will have sand and a few rocks on their bases, another may have some scrub land, and so on. You could also mark out officers and NCO's with a small flower or other detail on their bases; this renders them easily identifiable, without having to break the unification of a collection's appearance.

As we're covering figures fighting in the desert, it may seem that our choice of basing is pretty restricted. Luckily from our perspective, however, there is still plenty we can do to add a little visual interest to our bases, and a choice of different techniques open to us as well.

Being the desert, applying sand seems the most obvious way to do our desert bases. Sanding is also a long-standing and favourite way of adding texture to a wargames figure's base, and requires applying a layer of either superglue or PVA glue to the model's base, then sprinkling sand over it. Once this initial layer is dry, it's possible to either build up further levels of sand, for interest or to hide basing tabs. Do ensure you allow the previous layer to dry thoroughly for a few hours first though.

This Italian has had his base first coated with a fine modelling sand, then, once that had dried, had his base dry-brushed with some white paint. This may seem counterproductive, given that sand is usually the colour of sand, however when used with wargaming figures, even at the larger sizes, raw sand tends to resemble a shingle beach rather than a scorched desert. To counter this, we can either dry-brush the bases with white or Pale Sand to tone back the effect a little, or paint the base first with a darker

sand colour, then dry-brush a few lighter shades. Simply treat the base as painting any other part of the figure.

To give the impression of winter's mud, an effect especially appropriate for modelling figures serving in the winter of the Tunisian campaign, you can use high-end weathering products; however, a quick and effective method is to simply sand the base, and then paint it with the dark sand colour as shown further on in this guide. Once that has dried, give the base a coat of either soft tone or strong tone, and you have an easy and quick dark earthy-looking base, to which you can add gravel or static grass as you see fit.

Finally, an increasingly available group of products to hit the shelves are varying types of textured paint. These come in a variety of colours, and have either cracking mediums added to give the appearance of baked and cracked earth, or they come pre-mixed with microballs that will give the appearance of very fine sand once dry. These are my preferred tool for basing, as it combines both adding sand, as well as the initial layer of paint.

To apply texture paints, simply use an old brush, and apply the paint straight from the container to the base. You can apply the paint fairly thickly, and this is actually encouraged, especially with the crackle paints as these will dry to form deeper, and more prominent details. Once the texture is dry, you can then go on to dry-brush and add details as you wish.

For painting your bases, there are no hard and fast rules to what colours to use, however there is a very simple set of steps you can run through to add paint to them. We'll assume the base below has had the sand stuck down, and been allowed to dry overnight.

Step 1

In this step, we're simply painting a layer of a fairly dark sand paint over the base. You can of course pick any colour you like for this, I've chosen a colour with a pleasing contrast to the next stages.

Area	Paint used
Whole base	Vallejo 824 German Camouflage Orange

Step 2

Now, we'll give the base a fairly heavy dry-brushing of a medium sand colour; you do not need to worry about overloading the brush with paint as you normally would with dry-brushing, as the plan is to simply get a good layer of this mid-colour down.

Paints Used:

Area	Paint used
Whole base	Vallejo 916 Sand Yellow

Step 3

Finally, we give the brush a light dry-brush with some pure white. This will give a nice contrast with the previous colours, and feel like a fine, powdered sand. On to this you can go on to add any detail features you require.

Area	Paint used
Whole base	Vallejo 951 White

Adding Detail

With the base now painted, we can start to think about adding some extra interesting details. There is a

staggering array of products available for this purpose, and a trip to the model railway section of your local hobby shop will reveal some stunning scenic items.

For desert basing, I like to use some fine gravel, usually marketed for model railway ballast. This comes in black, grey and brown shades most commonly, and I tend to use each of them fairly equally. To attach the gravel, apply a few small dabs of superglue to your now-painted base, sprinkle or place a few small clusters of gravel onto the base, allow it to dry thoroughly, then give the brush a dry-brush of your final highlight colour

To add some scrub grass to your base, you can use either static grass, or pre-made clumps of foliage. Both

these products essentially perform the same function. Pre-made clumps are supplied on a backing sheet of paper, and are simply lifted from this sheet and stuck down to the base with a little PVA glue.

Static grass is supplied as loose strands, and can be purchased in varying lengths and pretty much any colour imaginable. I like to use yellow and brown tones for my desert basing purposes. To make a patch of scrub bush, simply paint a small blob of PVA onto the base then, using some tweezers, pick up a cluster and stick them onto the

base vertically. Wait for the glue to dry, then gently blow on the model to remove any excess grass.

The methods above are just a start to what you can achieve when basing your models, but will hopefully give you a few ideas to create some exciting and interesting effects for your desert projects. With so many different products and techniques available I could probably fill a volume simply discussing all the options and techniques possible, but most of them are essentially variations on what is covered here.

There are ranges of enamel and powdered weathering products that can give interesting effects, and are simply applied as one would a wash over a painted base. Different types of scatter can also be had, another favourite of mine

replicates wood and forest scatter, and can be applied using the same techniques as static grass. With basing, as with all techniques, it never hurts to experiment, and it can be quite handy to get some spare bases and use those to test out any ideas that present themselves to you for future use. Ultimately, and really with any aspect of the hobby, keep experimenting and have fun!

List of Manufacturers

With so many ranges and sizes of models to be had, it can be quite daunting attempting to find models to use with a project, especially something as well catered for as a North African campaign force from the Second World War. To hopefully make things a little easier, and also as a handy reference, here's a list of manufacturers, broken down into both size and what they produce.

This list is fairly exhaustive, but there is probably more that I've forgotten, and I'm also just listing those ranges directly suitable for the desert, as it's quite easy to incorporate other model ranges as well at times due to the extensive array of equipment worn and used. This should serve as a good starting point for you to expand your collections however!

Size: 28mm or 1/56 scale(ish)	Notes:
Warlord Games	Warlord produce several ranges of both metal and plastic figures, as well a very large range of vehicle models, again in metal or plastic depending on the popularity of the vehicle.
Artizan Designs	Wide range of metal figures.
Perry Miniatures	Both plastic and metal figures, resin vehicles.
Offensive Miniatures	Metal figures and vehicles.
Gothic Line miniatures	Metal figures.
Crusader Miniatures	Crusader have a range of metal Americans suitable for North Africa.
Black Tree Design	Extensive ranges of metal figures and vehicles.
Rubicon Models	Large range of plastic vehicles, with figures hinted at for the future.

Eureka Miniatures	Metal figures, including some fun character pieces.
Gorgon Miniatures	Metal figures.
Wargames Foundry	Metal figures.
Size: 20mm or 1/72 scale(ish)	**Notes:**
Plastic Soldier Company	Producers of both figures and vehicles in plastic, with a steadily growing range of metal figures becoming added to the line.
SHQ	Large range of metal figures and vehicles.
Steel 72	Small but growing range of figures.
Britannia Miniatures	Large range of resin vehicles, and metal figures.
Kelly's Heroes	Extensive range of metal figures.
Wartime Miniatures	Metal figures.
AB Miniatures	Steadily expanding range of metal figures.
Wargames Foundry	Metal figures.
Airfix	Plastic vehicles, and soft plastic figures.
Revell	Plastic vehicles, and soft plastic figures.
Italeri	Plastic vehicles, and soft plastic figures.
S Models	Plastic vehicles.
First to Fight	Plastic vehicles.
Underfire Miniatures	Metal figures.
Shellhole Scenics	Metal figures, and resin vehicles.
CP Models	Metal figures.
Early War Miniatures	Metal Figures.
Size: 15mm or 1/100(lsh)	**Notes:**
Battlefront	Very large range of models suitable for use with the desert campaigns. Models available in metal, resin and plastic.
Forged in Battle	Another large range of metal and resin models suitable for North Africa.

Peter Pig	Range of metal figures and vehicles.
Old Glory	Metal figures.
SkyTrex	Metal vehicles and figures.
Plastic Soldier Company	Very large range of plastic vehicles and good range of plastic figures.
Zvezda	Extensive range of plastic vehicles.